Smart Moves

SMART MOVES

SUCCESSFUL STRATEGIES AND TACTICS
FOR CAREER MANAGEMENT

GODFREY GOLZEN
& ANDREW GARNER

Basil Blackwell

Copyright © Godfrey Golzen and Andrew Garner, 1990

First published 1990

Published by Basil Blackwell in association with Penguin Books Ltd.

Basil Blackwell Ltd
108 Cowley Road, Oxford, OX4 1JF, UK

Basil Blackwell, Inc.
3 Cambridge Center
Cambridge, Massachusetts 02142, USA

British Library Cataloguing in Publication Data

A CIP catalogue record for this book is available from
the British Library.

Library of Congress Cataloging in Publication Data

Garner, Andrew.
Smart moves: successful strategies and tactics for career
management/Andrew Garner and Godfrey Golzen.
p.   cm.
ISBN 0-631-17233-5
1. Career development.   I. Golzen, Godfrey, 1930-   . II. Title.
HF5381.G294   1990
650.1-dc20   90-31257   CIP

Typeset in 12 on 13½ pt Joanna
by Joshua Associates Ltd, Oxford
Printed in Great Britain by
T. J. Press Ltd, Padstow, Cornwall

Contents

Acknowledgements

The seeds of this book lay in a concern that Andrew Garner developed in 1985 with the number of MBAs' C.V.s that crossed his desk that were associated with their careers going wrong instead of being fulfilled. Following contact with all leading business schools in Europe, a relationship was forged with Manchester Business School, and the concept of 'Career Management' was created. Since that time, the 10 week course for second year MBAs has escalated to become an examined subject and has attracted guest speakers from the highest echelons of industry and commerce. Our deep appreciation, therefore, goes to Alan Pearson, Dr Rab Telfer and latterly to Dr Tom Cannon whose shared vision has been of enormous encouragement. Thanks are also due to Andrew Garner's partners at the London office of Boyden International, Mile Curlewis, Peter Skala and David Hutt for pooling their wide ranging experience and contacts.

We would like to acknowledge the help of the many managers who spared time out of their busy lives to talk to us about their careers. That applies both to those named in the text and those who preferred to remain unattributed or asked for their name to be disguised, for reasons that will be obvious from the context in which they have been quoted.

We would also like to acknowledge three particular contributions: the very useful comments made at crucial stages of the book by Duncan Lewis, Director of Strategic Planning at Hawker Siddeley and by John Dunn, International Vice-President of Human Relations at EMI Music. In researching US sources and material, Godfrey Golzen also valued a meeting in Boston, Massachusetts, with the American organizational psychologist and consultant, Dr Fritz Steele. Chapter 8 on the relationship between corporate cultures and working environments owes much to his ideas on the subject.

It will be obvious to readers that we owe a considerable debt of gratitude to such key writers on organizational issues as Peter Drucker, Charles Handy, Roseabeth Moss Kanter and Tom Peters. In as far as this book is original, it is in matching their work to the day-to-day observations and wisdom of a headhunter and a management writer.

Godfrey Golzen
Andrew Garner

1

The Context:
That Uncertain Feeling

Careers can be viewed as fictions about the past to help us feel better about the future.' That was the conclusion reached by two psychologists from Sheffield University, Nigel Nicholson and Michael West, in their study of the career patterns of 2300 members of the British Institute of Management – a veritable Kinsey Report on how the turbulent business environment of the past decade has affected middle and senior managers.[1]

Their phrase produced an uneasy smile of recognition from everyone we talked to in the course of researching this book, because in fact very few people have a career plan that is anything more than a set of expedients.

That is odd. In all their other activities managers operate on a basis of business plans, forecasts and budgets. But when it came to managing their own careers, Nicholson and West found that in most cases, and at almost any level, careers were a set of improvizations based on loose assumptions about the future, rather than a coherent match between personal values and skills and corporate needs and goals. Typically, they are made up of some of the following ingredients:

- Opportunistic moves in the direction of money, promotion and job satisfaction – reading the job advertisements or talking to recruitment intermediaries in response to a gut feeling that the time is ripe to make a move, for whatever reason
- A blind belief that since everything has gone well so far, it will continue to do so in the future – in the light of the growing

unpredictability of the organizational environment, that may be compared to the cartoon of the man falling from a building and shouting 'OK, so far' to horrified spectators at a second-floor window
- Simple fatalism – a belief that careers are determined largely by luck, being in the right place at the right time with the right set of skills and competencies
- Faith that ability and achievement will be recognized and rewarded by the organizations they are already in

There is, of course, a devil's advocate argument for saying that a career is not something you can plan – that there are too many imponderables, uncertainties and variables involved. Another school of thought finds the idea of career planning, frankly, distasteful. Its adherents think of it in terms of the literature of rather primitive, prescriptive 'how to be a success' books and articles which tell you how to cultivate the right people, wear the right clothes, plan Machiavellian schemes for self-advancement, and so forth.

That is not our intention at all in writing this book. We do not believe that career management is a matter of following instructions, like reading a cookbook. But we do think it is important for people to plan their own career paths rather than leaving them to chance or relying on the organizations that employ them. Nor do we think that good career moves are necessarily ones which conform to some external criterion of what is regarded as success. One of our key arguments is that good career moves are those that enable people to find settings which enable them to do what they really want to. Since that usually also happens to be what they are best at, such moves meet both organizational and personal objectives.

Another point which is crucial to career management – but often overlooked – is finding the right fit between organizational culture and personal characteristics. Both of these are likely to be different at various stages of their life-cycles. A young organization, or one which is being rejuvenated by a turnaround chief executive, is a different place to work than a mature one. Similarly, a younger manager has different aspirations, attitudes and needs from those of an older person.

Part of our approach, therefore, is also to enable readers to make sense of organizations in ways which are relevant to good career moves. In writing about that, we have used – and we have not seen this attempt made anywhere else – the growing literature on 'corporate culture' and related it to career development. We have also made a connection between these two aspects and individual lifespan development. We have set out to show:

- How the culture and behaviour of organizations differ at various stages of their development
- How the people in them are likely to behave
- How to read and interpret the signs of that behaviour
- How eventually to make career moves that align one's own values, attributes, objectives and developmental stage with the organizational culture one is likely to be meeting

Nevertheless, the result is not a 'how to' book in the conventional sense, but a kit of parts, which can broadly be applied by those trying to find their way forward in the job market at a time when many of its old certainties and assumptions have been swept away: above all, that organizations will, at least to some degree, offer the kind of career patterns that they used to offer – advance the best; promote the good to their proper levels in the hierarchy; tuck away the not-so-good, or those perceived to be so, in some place where they cannot do much harm and, if they are still young enough, probably take the hint that they ought to look elsewhere. Charles Handy, in his book, The age of unreason,[2] invites readers to consider the proposition that 'we should stop thinking of employers and employment'. Certainly the signs are gathering that ownership of careers is being transferred from the organization to the individual. In a career sense we are all self-employed now. How to manage that process is the theme of this book.

The idea of writing a book like this seldom comes out of the blue. It is triggered off by an event or a series of events which suddenly make you look at your environment in a slightly different way and realize that other people must also be sharing that perception.

In our case, the triggering experience was rather more negative. It concerned a medium-sized, privately owned family company that one of us had worked in for a number of years. Through lack of investment, internal dissensions in the controlling families and that debilitating corporate disease, failure to keep up with the times, it began to run into trouble in the early 1980s, although to the employees it was still an agreeable place in which to work and one which inspired a good deal of loyalty.

Then, one day, it was sold to a conglomerate for several million pounds – nothing so unusual in that. The dramatic element was provided by the chairman and principal shareholder, who simply vanished overnight without a word of explanation to the staff about the new owners, and without so much as saying goodbye even to the most senior executives, some of whom had given his family a working lifetime of service. 'His father would have turned in his grave. He took his money and ran', one of them said. They were, of course, immediately exposed to a comprehensive change of corporate culture, and quite a few of them did not survive it for long in career terms.

Dramas about ownership changes are perhaps rare in quite this form, but dramas are also metaphors about general truths. Nothing, we thought, illustrated the weakening of ties, obligations and traditional loyalties between employers and employees quite as graphically as this one occurrence.

The trend cuts both ways, of course. As managers experience or read about dramatic changes in the corporate environment which affect their careers but which are outside their control – for instance, the 2500 job losses in the City after the stock market crash of 1987 – they are beginning to feel the need to break away from corporate ties and become more involved in self-management. The frequency with which people change jobs (of which more later) is a sign of that: so is the growth of self-employment on both sides of the Atlantic. Again, one occurrence, more dramatic than the statistics, brought this home to us. When the Sunday Times published an article about 'executive leasing', essentially a form of freelance management consultancy, the firms mentioned as agencies for this type of work were literally deluged with letters from executives who wanted more information about it. Some of them, certainly, were people on the job market. But a very significant proportion were employed in senior positions and these included main board directors of nationally known PLCs. The spur was not money and it certainly was not security. What they were interested in was autonomy – being their own person.

Yet another experience, however, brought home to us the fact that many managers are also very ill-equipped to handle job changes and can make disastrous career mistakes because of that. We are talking here about a person who would be regarded as a winner: top of his class at one of the world's leading business schools, he was offered a line management job with an international company – he turned the job down in favour of an offer from a big firm of management consultants. Certainly the prize was a tempting one. Part of it was a substantial golden 'hello' which would enable him to pay off the debts he had incurred in funding his MBA, but there was also a large salary and a prestige car. Headhunters warned him that he would find it very difficult to move back into line management from consultancy. They also judged that his personal style would not sit easily with this particular firm of consultants. And so it proved. Within three months he left, and then had the job of explaining in subsequent interviews what looked like a failure, although, as is usually the case in these circumstances, tissue rejection by the corporate culture was at the root of it. Eventually he did secure a job with a smaller, second-division firm; but he is probably out of the race as far as his objective of becoming a director, and ultimately chief executive, of a major company is concerned.

As any career counsellor will tell you, tissue rejection is the story behind much of their caseload. So much of what follows is about reading and interpreting corporate cultures, and assessing the alignment between the way they do things (still the best definition of that elusive concept) and the way you do things.

The post-feudal workplace

The perils of the 'not one of us' syndrome and how to avoid it by reading the corporate culture before you become part of it – not later, because by that time it may be too late – is one of the topics that we shall be examining. Another key issue is illustrated by the first of our two anecdotes.

We believe that it exemplifies the fundamental change that has occurred, perhaps only over the past ten years, in the relationship between employers and employees. We do not think that this is an isolated example of an abdication by weak or greedy management; nor do we think that owners cutting adrift is a temporary phenomenon to do with the difficulties of being a medium-sized player where only very large or very small organizations seem to survive economic uncertainty, the shift from manufacturing to service industries, the wave of mergers and acquisitions and so forth. All these are vital factors, but it is what they have caused that is the most significant thing.

It has conjured up forces that have changed the nature of the contract between organizations and the people who work in them. To describe the period which began in the early 1980s as the 'post-industrial age' is in fact to understate what has happened in the workplace. We see it as the most profound change in relationships between masters and men since feudalism. That is the subscript to a conversation one of us had recently with an older-style chief executive. 'I wonder why our people feel so little loyalty towards the firm these days', he asked rhetorically in discussing the loss of a promising young manager to a rival firm. Peter Drucker provides a clue to the answer: as he writes in *Industry Week*, 'Loyalty is a two way street. What top managers call disloyalty, middle management people call taking responsibility for one's family and career'.[3]

But let us explain more about the connection with feudalism. Feudalism was a medieval form of government under which each grade of subject undertook to protect the grade below it in exchange for certain services: the lords would contract to supply a given number of knights in battle to their prince, the knights would undertake to bring along their followers – mainly their tenants and servants – and the followers would agree to supply their labour to the knights, as well as their physical presence in war, in exchange for protection from marauders. In its legal, official form it broke down somewhere around the fifteenth century, but as a kind of understanding between employers as protection-givers and employees as service-renderers, it survived into the twentieth-century workplace. What employers, until recently, gave to employees, as well as money, was protection in the form of job security. The context was a stable business environment in which most employers observed a fairly fixed set of rules about the way in which they paid their staff.

Within reason, it did not matter whether they were doing the job well or not. Everyone aged over 45 will remember the dim but loyal corporate servants, or the demotivated middle managers parked in some corporate siding while the action moved on past them. Their jobs were secure and the money was not necessarily bad, because they were in a certain grade determined by length of service and ostensible seniority which nearly always put them above their younger fellows, however talented. What they had given to achieve that situation was loyalty, the currency of feudalism.

Nobody wants it now. The new word on the unwritten contract is 'commitment'; commitment to the job in hand through a total focus of abilities and energies, the quality of which is under constant scrutiny. But little importance is attached to loyalty to the employer as an entity. The point is clearly made by Tim Bell, of the advertising agency Lowe, Howard-Spink and Bell, in an interview quoted in *The hundred best companies to work for in the UK*:[4]

> We don't give people a career, we give them a job. Every day is an opportunity to prove that you should be given a chance or that your work is better than the next guy's. It is competitive. It is tough. No one is going to do you any favours. Ultimately your only loyalty will be to yourself.

A similar view is expressed by John Sculley, President of Apple Computers, in his book, *Odyssey*.[5] Within what he regards as the organizations of the future – knowledge-oriented, loosely structured companies such as Apple:

> You are asked to pour a part of yourself into the success of the company . . . in many ways the individual is asked for a greater commitment than in the days when he or she was simply a cog

in the wheel of a systematised corporation. In return, you should get an experience that sharpens your instincts, teaches you the newest lessons, shows you how to become self-engaged in your work, gives you new ways of looking at the world. ... I'm not asking for open ended loyalty. I am asking people who are at Apple to buy in to the vision of the company while they are here.

Such sentiments are echoed by Jack Welch, President of General Electric, a huge but agile American conglomerate that is often held up as a model for big business in the 1990s: 'GE will make no promises about lifetime employment, but it will be a challenging place to work and will enhance workers' skills so that they can find other jobs if the company no longer needs them', he told the US magazine *Business Week*.

There are some interesting analogies between this change of attitude to the nature of employment and the decline of feudalism. Feudalism as a system could not handle the rise of cities, with their entrepreneurial middle class and their fragmented social networks. Neither of these fitted into what had previously been the ordained order of things. In a similar way, the kind of organizations that existed up to the end of the 1970s have been increasingly unable to keep what Peter Drucker has termed 'knowledge workers' within a traditional organizational frame: highly skilled technical specialists, those with professional qualifications or with particular areas of expertise related to a product or a market – or those with outstanding talents as managers. These people are no longer prepared to make the long, slow march up the organizational hierarchy.

One reason for that is that organizations can no longer protect them while they are doing it, any more than feudalism could protect its subjects when it came to the rise of national, as compared to local, power. Feudal lords could shield their subjects from robber barons, but not from major wars and invasions. In the same way, employers can no longer protect their workforce from the consequences of hostile takeovers, from pressure from institutional shareholders who are now, with the help of information technology, able to look globally and daily for maximum returns –

and above all from the effects of the pace of change itself. Already, in 1987, a televised discussion on the future of organizations made the point that 75 per cent of all products or services on the market at that time were new, or being offered in a different form from ten years previously. The effect of that is that skills which are in great demand in one phase may be rendered obsolete by the next advance in technology.

The response of organizations has, to a greater or lesser degree, been to change the nature of the 'contract' with the people who work for them. Again, Sculley puts it well in his book. Talking of past and present relationships within organizations, he says:

> The bond between man and institutions represented a social contract in which the Organisation Man traded his loyalty for security and lifetime employment. It was a Faustian bargain which seemed to offer the jobholder limitless wishes, while robbing him of his freedom, his motivation, his creativity.
>
> That social contract is no longer valid. Nor, perhaps, should it be. ... The trappings of loyalty – pension, cradle to grave employment – have been replaced by such things as creating opportunity, rewards and challenges for people.

What he means is that the ingredients of the 'contract' are no longer the feudal ones of job security and a career path owned by the organization. There is a new set of contents: tools to enable you to manage your own career (and not much else, in some organizations). The rest is up to you.

Tools for personal career management

Training and development

Knowledge and skills do not date as rapidly as manufactured products, but they can become obsolete over a relatively short time because of the quickening pace of technological change. Certainly they have a limited shelf life, and this applies even to professional qualifications. A report by the British Institute of Management[6] makes the point that the role of professional bodies in the future may be more to provide continuing development than to act as guardians of a 'meal ticket' qualification:

> Membership of a professional association may in future come to be associated rather more with securing (perhaps temporary) access to a relevant range of professional services and less as an indication of having undergone a preparation for a lifetime career.

That applies, if anything even more so, to the kind of technological skills that are currently in strongest worldwide demand. 'In some areas of electronics', a report by the National Economic Development Council tells us, 'there is a saying that the "half-life" of PhDs is only about four or five years – in other words that fully half of what they know will be out of date by then.'[7]

That has important career implications. Tom Peters, whose books and lectures have made him the successor to Peter Drucker as the world's most influential thinker on management matters, says that organizations are essentially devices for processing information and knowledge. Therefore it is the possession of knowledge and the control of information that confers power in organizations, not roles or titles.

That point was grasped, usually instinctively, by middle management in the feudal workplace. Middle management either had bits of knowledge, for instance about production techniques, which they kept to themselves and guarded zealously; or they acted as filters for information as it moved laboriously up and down the organization. Tom Peters, for instance, tells of one US car company in which any spending decision over $1 m needed 44 signatures. Each of the signatories, who included people not at all prominent in the hierarchy, had power – that was their 'piece of the action'.

Two factors have served to change that. One is that information technology means that information is no longer accessed through a filter of intermediaries but is 'main-lined' to managers through the VDU on their desk. For instance, EPOS (electronic point of sale) devices allow them to track the daily movement of goods through the checkout points in the shops, rather than wait for weekly or monthly reports – filtered through and sometimes massaged by a host of intermediaries. The second factor is that information technology also means that knowledge can be shared across boundaries to a greater extent. The VDU can be a window as well as a screen.

But you have to work at it to take advantage of that fact. Rather than expanding roles upwards, you have to extend your knowledge sideways, both informally through contacts with colleagues who are willing to share their knowledge and formally through training. The organizations that provide opportunities to enhance knowledge and to update skills are 'learning organizations'. They play a vital career role because, as Rosabeth Moss Kanter has recently put it: 'If security no longer comes from being employed, then it must come from being employable'.[8] We shall devote some space to how to identify them in making a career move.

Money

Rewards in real terms are greater than they have ever been at every level of the private sector, but they are being assembled in a different way. Instead of grades, there are market rates and 'golden hellos' – premiums paid to stars, like transfer fees in football. Instead of annual increments there are profit-sharing schemes, share options which give employees a piece of the action and, in some cases, twice-yearly reviews to keep up with fast-moving reward sectors. Above all, there is performance-based pay. Together, these elements now account for 50 per cent and more of most executive pay packages.

This means that the relationship between employer and employee is becoming more like that of partners collaborating towards a mutually beneficial end than that of masters and servants. That situation has been officially recognized in the UK by the extension of tax concessions to personal pension schemes for employees, instead of just to the self-employed. That clearly signals the transfer of career management responsibility to the individual. As we said earlier, in career terms, everyone is now self-employed.

Even the relationship between hourly-paid workers and managers is changing with the spread of employee share

ownership schemes, which give general access to what used to be
regarded as the company's secrets. Information technology also
plays a role here. Corporate 'big brothers' can measure each individual's contribution with greater accuracy than before: but information technology also enables individuals to watch big brother.

However, autonomy has a price on it. These new relationships
are not at all like those between partners in professional practice:
'gentlemen in business', as one commentator has described them,
bound together at least until irreconcilable differences do them
part – although even that is changing. The new, post-feudal arrangements last only as long as they are convenient, useful or as circumstances permit. They are arbitrarily dissolved by changes of fortune,
as happened in many financial institutions after the 'Black Monday'
stock market crash of 1987, or when the skills of one party are no
longer quite so useful to the other party as they were, and there is
nowhere else in the organization where they can be applied.

On the positive side, it is now less true than it was to say that
'you can't make money working for someone else'. A 1989 survey,
by Labour Research, showed that some 2000 directors in the UK
were earning £100 000 or more, and that 36 of these were earning
over £500 000.⁹ Rewards at this level are quite common in some
of our competitor economies. The skills shortage and the global
nature of the employment market make it probable that there will
continue to be an upward drift in financial rewards in all industrialized countries and at all levels. But money is not just a reward
and an attraction. It is also a career tool in the sense that it buys
the freedom to consider wider options, such as the possibility of
becoming independent at a later stage in one's career or taking a
year out to enhance personal development in the earlier stages.
There is, in fact, a growing connection between financial planning
and career planning. Money, as we are always told, is not everything. In careers, it should be accompanied either by scope for
personal development or by our third tool, visibility.

Visibility

The term 'visibility' is beginning to appear more and more in
recruitment advertisements as one of the attractions of a job. The

reason is that it is the factor which enables you to control and attract the next set of events in your own career. It means that the nature of the job is such that what you achieve in it will mark you out as a manager who has had some visible impact on the organization as a whole. As Rosabeth Moss Kanter found in her fascinating study of what really happens in organizations, Men and women of the corporation,[10] 'People who looked like "comers" seemed to have instinct for doing the visible'.

Visibility means more than recognition. It embraces the wider notion of 'reputation'. Recognition is what you get within the organization for a job well done, but it is not necessarily negotiable currency in the world outside. In his survey of 144 senior directors of UK companies, Developing top managers,[11] Professor Alan Mumford found that the reason why they thought colleagues 'with apparently equal experience and ability' had not made it was because 'their job had very low visibility and excellent performance was simply not noted'. To achieve, in the laboratory or in the marketplace, a 2–3 per cent improvement in the performance of a nationally established brand, for instance, may have a considerable internal effect and mark you out as a coming executive within that one organization. But it does not have the same impact in the wider world as being involved in a new product launch, with all the publicity that engenders. That would give you visibility, as well as recognition.

Visibility is what makes you noticed more widely, notably by headhunters, or executive search consultants, to give them their proper name. They now play an increasingly important role when it comes to making senior and specialized appointments, or even in picking out high-flyers at the beginning of their careers. For instance, when lists are published of the people who pass professional examinations with distinction, they find their way into the headhunters' files. Some graduates receive offers before they have even started to look for a job themselves.

Visibility to the external world is more difficult to achieve in large, established companies than in small ones – so does that indicate that small companies are the ones to go for? Opinions are divided about this. According to some headhunters, the large companies that retain them often specify that line management candidates must come from a similar corporate environment; rather in the same way that football clubs in the first division look for players in first-, not third- or fourth-division clubs. There is, they say, a qualitative difference between the game as it is played at different levels. That indicates that those who want to get to the top as a line manager in one of the larger companies will have to make an appropriate career decision early on. But they will also have to ensure that they position themselves in roles in which they can add value in visible ways: being involved in turnaround ventures or new product launches are two typical ways of doing this.

On the other hand, there are many who maintain that the all-round experience that comes with being a line manager in a smaller firm is the best form of training that there is. In the future, the drive to develop a more entrepreneurial spirit in all organizations may well tilt the balance towards achieving a mix between large- and small-company experience in the crucial early stages of a career. But in all cases you have to be a recognizable face in the crowd.

Avoiding the checkmate move

Instinctively, managers have already grasped the need to make career moves that offer the opportunity to develop these tools for career management. One of the characteristics of the post-feudal workplace is that, in search of opportunities, managers move from job to job much more frequently than they did even a decade ago. In their study of the career patterns of 2300 members of the British Institute of Management, Nicholson and West found that 'three years is the average duration of job tenure, though there is wide variation around this average: as many as one in ten have had five or more jobs in the last five years'. Most of these moves, incidentally, occurred between the start of working life and the mid-thirties.

Clearly, managers feel there is an advantage in making such moves and the survey suggested they are right. From their data on careers, the authors concluded that 'There is an unmistakeable implication ... that if you want to get on in management, you would be advised to change organisations from time to time'. But it is not quite as simple as that.

Just as, in chess, there are moves which seem like good ideas at the time, but eventually turn out to be fatal mistakes, from a career management point of view there are some perils in manoeuvring for position without thinking about where this will leave you. Of the moves that were charted by Nicholson and West, 50 per cent fell into the category of what the authors described as 'upward spiralling' – out, upwards and functionally sideways from a larger to a smaller organization. Those who had done this seemed to feel they would be given more scope in such a setting. Equally, small firms are keen to recruit executives with big-company experience.

The career trap for those on the way up is that it is then very difficult to move back from a small company to a large one. All headhunters agree that, certainly at present, big companies want general managers with a predominantly big-company background, preferably in what they call an 'academy company'. By that they mean a firm that is highly regarded in its industry and that provides its employees with a range of transferable skills, experiences and contacts: Mars and IBM would be typical examples. Visibility, therefore, is not about being a big fish in a small pond – unless that is what you want to be.

It is also not about achievement in a purely staff role.[12] For this reason, it is very difficult to move from consultancy to line management. The analytical skills involved in consultancy seem to be regarded as essentially those of a staff function, and these are felt to be of a different order from those required by managers.

This may change, but the evidence so far suggests that there are a number of distinct career paths for those with ambitions to get to the top. Those who want to do so in a large corporate setting will have to set their course in line management there quite early on, although the option to spiral outwards to a smaller organization remains open until quite late in the career. But if you move into a smaller organization early after about age 30, that is likely to limit your chance of getting to the top in a large one.

Large organizations who want to keep their star players are aware of the fact that, by definition, self-development is part of their career agenda. Therefore they try to provide opportunities for them to fill a number of functional roles; for instance, to move them from finance into human resources or marketing or to provide the opportunity to manage an operation overseas. The person who is determined to make his or her career within one organization has to consider very carefully whose interests are served by such opportunities, so we will deal with where to strike the balance of such interests. It must be said that the conclusions of the Sheffield survey are unequivocal: 'Simply experiencing a series of promotions within an organisation is less likely to lead to the top . . . the manager moving to a new organisation is in a better bargaining relationship with the new employer, and has greater leverage for status rewards than does the intra-organisational mover'.

The view from the plateau – is it so poor?

Plateauing has had a very bad press in career literature. A typical example is the definition given in a report on the subject produced by Sundridge Park Management Centre:[13] 'Managers whose expertise is needed by their company, but for whom there are no further prospects in terms of promotion or advancement'.

However, the fact has to be faced that in the post-feudal organization, shaped more like a rather flat pyramid than the multi-runged ladder of the past, the opportunities for 'advancement' in the traditional sense will be far fewer. Professor Charles Handy, whose views on the future of work, first expressed in a book of that name in 1984,[14] have proved remarkably accurate, said at a conference in London in 1988 that he foresaw organizations of the future as having a hierarchical structure more like that of a university, with only four grades of seniority. That view is borne out by what is already happening in the USA. According to Tom Peters, Wal-Mart, America's most successful retail operation with sales of over $15 bn and 1000 stores, is run from a small office with only three levels of management.

This means that we may have to take a different view of

the course of careers. Speaking in London in 1989, Peters drew a parallel with acting. 'Only a very few actors can be big stars', he said: 'The rest have to learn to play many different roles in the course of their working lives and to accept the fact that they perform better in some than in others'.

But if structural plateauing is inevitable, this is not true of content plateauing or personal plateauing. The reason why the whole process is viewed with such alarm is that the three are usually confused with each other. Content plateauing occurs when you feel there is nothing more to the job – boredom, in other words. Personal plateauing, with which it is often associated, is when you feel that life has no new and exciting experiences to offer. The way to avoid both these problems is to work across the structural plateau towards developing personal skills, and contacts and ranges of experience with others at the same level. 'There's nothing wrong with a plateau if it gives you enough room to expand your experience and knowledge', says Tom Peters.

But what about the aim with which we've all grown up – getting to the top? The simple fact that has to be faced here is that there are fewer places at or near the top in the pyramid than there were on the ladder. There is also a growing recognition, both by individuals and organizations, that getting to the top is not the only game in town. To begin with, very few people are intellectually and psychologically equipped to play it (we will deal with some of their attributes in a later chapter) or to make the sacrifices it entails. When ICI began to run their career workshops for managers, for instance, they discovered that only a tiny minority had large corporate ambitions. Most of them were more interested in doing jobs that fulfilled personal goals. That is a characteristic of the post-feudal knowledge worker: most of ICI's employees are graduates and we were told that so many of them also have PhDs that they no longer bother to put that fact on their visiting cards. The knowledge worker has goals that are determined from within, rather than by structures outside themselves. Organizations that grasp this fact have also found the answer to the 'Peter principle' of promoting people beyond the level of their abilities.

Career women as role models

Structural plateauing is a phenomenon with which women managers in organizations are all too familiar. According to a report produced by Ashridge Management College,[15] fewer than 3 per cent of the directors of the top 1500 UK companies are women, although they account for 45 per cent of the workforce. The situation is the same in the USA, where only 0.8 per cent of the women in the Fortune 1000 companies hold top positions.

There is, of course, no overt discrimination against women because that is illegal. Kathryn Riley, personnel director of County Natwest and one of the few female top executives in the City, describes the situation as the 'glass ceiling effect': 'You can't see the barriers that keep women from the top, but they're there all right and you know when you've hit them', she told us. They take the form of invisible but rigid barriers; for instance, in the form of the male-dominated club culture that persists in some City firms and where many key decisions are still made. 'Men are still more comfortable with other men,' writes F. N. Schwartz in the *Harvard Business Review*: 'As a result women miss many of the career opportunities that arise over lunch, on the golf course, or in the locker room'.[16]

It becomes, in some cases, a classic Catch 22. Women cannot secure top jobs because they lack relevant experience: but they cannot secure the key positions that would open the way there because they are women. That applies particularly to running an overseas subsidiary, a standard stop on the route for high-flyers.

Like other women managers to whom we spoke, Ms Riley made the point that women have to be better at their jobs than their male counterparts to succeed at every level. That has, however, led them to think more deeply about their careers. A report by Valerie Hammond of Ashridge Management College tells, for instance, that at British Rail women managers were directed into staff roles, whereas the road to higher responsibilities was clearly through line management. Women who wanted to advance to these levels had to 'insist on wider options at very early stages in their careers'.[17]

They also have to decide quite early on whether success, in

traditional terms, is really worth it; because the evidence is that it calls for enormous personal sacrifices. According to an article by Judi Marshall in the *Handbook of management development*,[18] 39 per cent of UK women managers are unmarried, divorced or widowed, as against 8 per cent of men. A similar situation is found in the USA. That has caused women to think harder than we suspect most men do about their personal values and priorities in relation to their career aspirations. It has also been suggested that the growth in self-employment among women – it is much greater than among men – is due to the fact that they are more aware of the need to define work, success and personal priorities on terms which they themselves set.

Secondly, the existence of the 'glass ceiling' and the knowledge, for women, that most of them are on a plateau of some kind, has produced exactly the kind of behaviour that we suggest is right for the post-feudal workplace. According to Ms Riley, they are more supportive of each other, more ready to collaborate rather than compete, and more ready to adapt to change. Nicholson and West found they are also 'more interested in fulfilling the need for growth' and 'more self-directed and intrinsically motivated in career choices'. There are, of course, those who deny that women's management style is any different from that of men, but few would agree with that on the evidence.

One aspect that seems to play a significant role in women's careers is both giving and accepting mentoring. This is interesting because Professor Mumford, in his survey of British managers, found that mentor relationships have not played much of a part in their development and concluded that it was 'much less present than recent literature suggests'.

By contrast, Pascale and Athos, in their widely discussed book, *The art of Japanese management*,[19] point out how Japanese managers develop quite strong mentoring relationships with close subordinates. In the course of these, they have no inhibitions about admitting to their own shortcomings and even failures, and see such exchanges as an essential part of developing themselves as well as those they are mentoring. In the West, admissions of weakness by superiors towards subordinates are usually regarded very negatively.

Pascale and Athos make the interesting suggestion that one of the reasons why women managers have not made a lot of headway in the West is precisely because the nurturing, sharing and mentoring role which, research indicates, is the way women work[20] is regarded with a good deal of suspicion in Western organizations, despite the lip service paid to its virtues by writers on human resource management.

Demographic trends in many Western countries point very clearly to the fact that women will play a much greater role in management in the coming decades. For instance, in the UK the number of entrants into the job market by the mid-1990s will have declined by 30 per cent, and in Germany by 43 per cent. Organizations will simply have to attract more women; and if they want to keep them, they will have to make concessions to the way women prefer to work. But as we have already said, this also fits in with the way in which the post-feudal workplace operates. The great success of a number of women entrepreneurs – not to mention women political leaders – is a sign that, perhaps intuitively, women have already grasped many of its realities. But intuition itself, not highly regarded by managers in the past, forms part of a competitive edge when information technology makes facts freely available.

Executive summary

It is said that when Louis XVI saw the mob on its way to the storming of the Bastille in 1789, he turned to one of his courtiers and said, 'Sir, this is a revolt'; to which the courtier replied, 'Sire, it is not a revolt. It is the revolution'. Revolutions are hard to recognize until historians write about them after the event, but commentators are generally agreed that the effects of the spread of information technology have changed the structure of the workplace and the relations between people at work in a revolutionary way, which also profoundly affects careers.

All work, as Peter Drucker has pointed out, is increasingly becoming knowledge work[21] and he comments that: 'there are no "higher" or "lower" knowledges. Knowledge is either relevant to a given task or irrelevant to it. The task decides, not the name, the age, the budget or the discipline.'

In other words, what is important for most people is going to be the amount of knowledge and skill they have, not their place in the pecking order. In another article, Drucker compares the new organization, which we have called 'post-feudal', to an orchestra. You enhance your value primarily by becoming a better player of your instrument; moving, if necessary, to a setting that allows you to do that. If you aim to become a conductor, you will also have to learn something about the other instruments – perhaps by attaching yourself to another section of the orchestra to learn its skills as well as your own core ones. However, there are not as many openings for conductors as there are for section leaders. It should also be noted that not many conductors come up through the orchestra, which points to a flaw in Drucker's metaphor.

Information technology impersonalizes the control of organizations and makes them the subject of the short-term views of the market and its makers rather than the longer perspective of ownership patronage. Employers (feudal lords) are no longer able to protect the interests of their employees (subjects). That means that employees are less willing to give loyalty to their employers: or at least not the same kind of loyalty. One can compare the new relationship to that of footballers, who give maximum performance to their clubs, but with one eye on their value in the transfer market.

The shift, in the post-feudal workplace, of the ownership of careers from the organization to the individual means that managers – and indeed all members of organizations – have to develop a new skill: the management of their own careers. Part of the input to that is 'hard': obtaining the tools, which we have described as career development, visibility and money.

Another part of it is 'soft'. It is concerned with changing attitudes towards careers in general, in particular with the recognition that, for all but a very few, the post-feudal career is not progress up a ladder but a journey across a series of settings which meet their career and personal expectations at various stages of life. That implies an ability to 'read' settings that are likely to meet those expectations. It also implies a readiness to analyse one's own needs, strengths, weaknesses and priorities; something many people are reluctant to face in the macho-traditional culture in which 'getting to the top', or at any rate up the ladder, was the name of the game.

We have suggested that women may be better at this new way of working than men because their expectations of getting up the ladder have always been limited and because they have always had to make choices about priorities. They have been better at working effectively across plateaux than men. Plateaux have had a bad press in career literature, but we think they have a bright future if you look at them, instead, as sections of an orchestra. Learning how to play with other members of the section is an essential skill – even for future conductors. For careers of the future, even those of high-flyers, we might have to turn Professor Higgins's cry on its head, and ask: 'Why can't a man be more like a woman?'

Notes

1 N. Nicholson and M. West, *Managerial job change: men and women in transition* (Cambridge University Press, 1988).
2 C. Handy, *The age of unreason* (Hutchinson, London, 1989).
3 P. Drucker, 'Tomorrow's restless managers', *Industry Week*, 18 April 1988.
4 Bob Reynolds, *The hundred best companies to work for in the UK* (Collins/ Fontana, London, 1989).
5 J. Sculley, *Odyssey: Pepsi to Apple* (Harper & Row, New York, 1987).
6 C. J. Coulson-Thomas, *The 'new professionals'* (British Institute of Management, Corby, Northants, UK, 1988).
7 J. Fairhead, *Design for corporate culture* (NEDO, London, 1987).
8 R. M. Kanter, *When giants learn to dance* (Simon & Schuster, New York and London, 1989).
9 *The Times*, 3 August 1989.
10 R. M. Kanter, *Men and women of the corporation* (Basic Books, New York, 1979).
11 A. Mumford, *Developing top managers* (Gower, Aldershot, Hants, UK, 1988).
12 Broadly speaking, the distinction between line and staff management is that the former carries with it direct responsibility for

bottom-line profit. Staff management is concerned primarily with internal services, such as R & D finance, human resources, etc.

13 Y. Deighan, *The plateaued manager* (Sundridge Park Management Centre, Croydon, UK, 1985).

14 C. Handy, *The future of work* (Basil Blackwell, Oxford, 1984).

15 Ashridge Management College, *Women in management* (Ashridge Management College, Berkhamsted, Herts, UK, 1988).

16 'Management women and the new facts of life', *Harvard Business Review*, January–February 1989.

17 V. Hammond, *Women in management in Great Britain* (Ashridge Management College, Berkhamsted, Herts, UK, 1987).

18 A. Mumford (ed.), *Handbook of management development*, 2nd edn (Gower, Aldershot, Hants, UK, 1986).

19 R. Pascale and A. Athos, *The art of Japanese management* (Penguin, London, 1986).

20 J. Marshall, *Women managers* (John Wiley, Chichester, 1984).

21 P. Drucker, *The age of discontinuity* (Heinemann, London/Harper & Row, New York, 1969).

2

Old Myths, New Realities

Change, as the example of Louis XVI shows, is difficult to recognize when you are living through it because it is usually deceptively gradual. As far as the working environment is concerned, if someone ten years ago had suddenly been translated to the workplace of today, they would have been stunned by the amount of information technology hardware now to be seen in virtually every office. But because this has happened over a period, many people have been able to live alongside it without adjusting to its many implications. There is a gruesome story, one hopes apocryphal, about an experiment carried out on frogs. They were put in water which was very gradually heated until it was boiling. The frogs died because their body mechanisms did not send out warnings about the effects on it of very small temperature changes.

The caseloads of career counselling firms are full of frogs: people who did not respond to change and who clung to old myths instead of recognizing new realities. You do not have to be a corporate senior citizen to fall into this trap either. The career of anyone over 35, at any level, has largely been formed by old myths.

The new realities are not secret. You can read about them in the newspapers every day. Smart moves are made by people who recognize them. Frogs either fail to draw the right inferences from the fact that the temperature is changing; or they jump without looking to see where they are going to land.

OLD MYTH   *There are some institutions and organizations that are so large and stable that they will not change in the foreseeable future.*

NEW REALITY   The ultimates in stability (and some would say career boredom) used to be the public-sector organizations. In one way or another, they now have to respond to market forces, not to a set of rules that they themselves make. That means they have to behave more like public companies – in fact many public-sector bodies in the UK have become that – by making a profit. They now offer greater rewards and benefits to their employees, but much diminished security. In fact, in many cases lifetime employment has been replaced by short-term contracts over 3–5 years.

This is not necessarily a temporary blip due to the ideology of the British Government of the day. When we discussed the matter with the highly respected former Director of the CBI, Sir Terence Beckett, he made the point that the speed with which information technology makes it possible to shift money around the world is also making it increasingly difficult for governments everywhere to collect taxes in order to finance public-sector deficits. Thus socialist New Zealand has, in 1989, gone as far down the privatization road as Conservative Britain. The other factor is that people seem to respond to the profit motive by delivering greater efficiency. In the Soviet Union, Mr Abel Abanbegyan was reported by The Economist[1] as saying: 'There is now an embryo financial market. Certain enterprises are introducing shares, stock and certificates'.

In the stability league the public sector has been just ahead of banks and financial institutions. But they have been profoundly influenced by competition – and again by the introduction of information technology. The banks are now competing for customers with building societies, and the building societies have swallowed up estate agencies in the recognition that providing financial services is an important part of what they actually do. In Norway, bank tellers are being retrained to become advisers on clients' personal finance, and counter services are being replaced by mechanical cash dispensers and acceptors.

In the private sector itself, the whole situation is summed up in Tom Peters' warning in his book, Thriving on chaos:[2] 'the "champ to chump" cycles are growing ever shorter'. A classic example is the one given in Megamistakes[3] of the world's leading slide rule manufacturer who, in 1967, failed to foresee the threat from electronic calculators: it wiped them out within a couple of years. Conversely, the 'chump to champ cycle' is also a phenomenon to be watched: a prime example was the way the Swiss watch industry, on its knees as a result of competition from digital watches, a technical innovation it had not anticipated, decided on the classic strategy of 'if you can't beat them, join them'. It swept the market with the 'Swatch', which turned a luxury item into a fashion accessory.

The 'chump to champ' cycle is the logic that fuels management buy-outs and has made a considerable number of individual fortunes.

CAREER MORAL **Everywhere you look there are both career threats and opportunities. For instance, the move towards mergers resulting in bigger and bigger corporate and professional units is a threat, both absolutely and in terms of limiting room at the top. But it is also a career opportunity in that some clients and customers will take their business away to smaller and more flexible enterprises, who in turn will need managers and entrepreneurs – preferably ones with relevant experience.**

OLD MYTH *Growth areas of the economy, or those with skill shortages, are the ones you can't go wrong with.*

NEW REALITY Changes are increasingly unpredictable – and they happen much faster than they used to. 'In some parts of the electronics industry', a 1987 NEDO report[4] tells us, '50% of sales revenue comes from products that did not exist 3 years ago'.

That process applies to skills as well as products. Take systems engineers in the electronics industry. In 1989 they were among the most highly paid specialists in their field and earned nearly twice as much as analyst programmers. But analyst programmers were top of the heap 4–5 years previous to that. Systems engineers will have to focus on different skills or run the risk of being replaced by the increasing smartness of the systems that are being devised all the time – by their peer–competitors.

Alternatively, take the City. Traders were sacked by the score after the stock market crash of 1987, and then lured back when the market recovered in the winter of 1988/9. But a report on the likely shape of the business environment in the year 2000, commissioned by Hay Management Consultants,[5] says that the increasing automation of trading 'will lead to a downgrading of the human trader both in image and in earning power terms'.

It is not, of course, only technology that creates uncertainty – although it does transmit it with alarming speed and efficiency. Currency movements, political upheavals, environmental changes, international competition in markets which firms used to regard as their home patch and the 'global village' effect of television publicity, foreseen by the almost forgotten 1960s guru Marshall McLuhan, issues such as the great salmonella food scare in the UK in 1988-9, can all change what appears to be a stable career environment very suddenly.

CAREER MORAL **Technology, more than projections of economic or demographic trends, drives the employment market.**

OLD MYTH *Qualifications are forever.*

NEW REALITY In the previous chapter, we referred to Colin Coulson-Thomas's report for the BIM on The *'new professionals'*. The core of his argument is that:

A more dynamic environment, the spread of expert systems and wider access to and availability of databases is likely to challenge the role of the 'professional' or 'expert' and greatly increase the importance of continuing education and updating.

That is confirmed by John Seear of the Institute of Chartered Accountants. Many of his members who have gone into industry have found that in career terms their hard-won qualifications are increasingly tarnished by the passage of time.

Within professional practices themselves, a further challenge is growing competition as the result of de-regulation. Lawyers are moving into areas such as mergers and acquisitions, which used to be reserved for merchant bankers; accountants are competing with management consultants; designers are challenging architects; and so on. In each case the competitive edge is that of new expertise in some field in which the traditional stakeholders thought they were well established.

The classic late-1980s route to what appears to be an ironclad management qualification is an MBA. We have nothing against MBAs. We think they are a very good thing, and the evidence is that those who take them are able to recoup their hard work, and often financial sacrifice, by achieving an immediate and dramatic increase in their earning power. But we think that as MBAs become less rare, their value in career-building terms will diminish. The question will be asked: Where and when did you take your degree? In America, for instance, where 25 per cent of all students now take some kind of business qualification, only about six MBA-awarding institutions (Harvard, MIT, Stanford Wharton Kellogg and Columbia) are taken seriously by major employers. 'When' is also a relevant question, because in recent years the reputation of some UK business schools has varied widely, with the appearance and disappearance of key professors.

But even if you attend one of the blue-chip institutes, careers will have to be planned around the knowledge that, as the BIM Report states, 'professional qualifications, without continuing education and professional updating (will) become regarded as having a definite "shelf life"'.

CAREER MORAL   **Today's hot ticket won't get you into to-morrow's show.**

OLD MYTH   *It's a good sign when you can map your future in an organization.*

NEW REALITY   We agree with Nicholson and West who say that 'only managers in stable, not to say stagnant environments have an accurate view of their futures'. At least, they think they have. It is precisely such organizations that are at risk from takeovers, and those who do not have or have not obtained transferable skills are then in great danger. A report produced on the consequences of acquisitions by the headhunters Egon Zehnder and the London Business School[6] confirms the impression that, particularly at senior levels, job losses can be severe. Within a year of such an event the average turnover of directors was 27 per cent.

CAREER MORAL   Don't believe the 'jam tomorrow' argument in a
career move that doesn't offer at least two out of three tools for
career management. The organizations that seem most stable and
therefore most in a position, apparently, to make promises to be
redeemed in the longer term are often the ones that are most
vulnerable.

OLD MYTH   *The way to the top here is through marketing, finance, production'*
or whatever.

NEW REALITY   There is some truth in the belief that the way to
the top in an organization is often dominated by one group,
individual or set of interests. But things can change very quickly.

- The direction of a business can be shifted abruptly by mergers
  and acquisitions or by policy changes. In 1988, for instance, the
  Maxwell Communication Corporation moved out of printing,
  which had been its core business, to focus on publishing. In the
  space of one person's working lifetime, Grand Metropolitan
  went from being a property company to being a hotel group
  and then an international food and drink conglomerate. At each
  stage, it sold off its previous core business: 'Within six months
  of this year [1988] it sold 800 pubs and put its chain of Inter-
  Continental hotels on the block. With the proceeds its seems to
  want buy brands, of everything from Irish whiskey to con-
  fectionery.'[7] That is happening even in small companies. In
  Edinburgh, an old established football team, Hibernians, is now
  a leisure-based public company with investments in hotels in
  the West of England.
- Today's important activity can be tomorrow's dead end, or vice
  versa. Research and development, which in many British firms
  used to be a place for parking bright misfits, has become vital
  for survival in manufacturing. In the USA the international
  division used to be a corporate graveyard. Now it is the place
  where they send the high-flyers.
- There is overwhelming evidence that the path upwards is no
  longer a single track. 'It is generally thought desirable that
  managers should have a range of functional experience before
  they reach the top' says Professor Mumford.[8] That means more

than just doing the same job under different circumstances: it means finance people doing a spell in marketing, sales executives getting involved in human resource management, and so forth. However, if you want to get to or near the top in a big company you will have to stay with big companies, and probably with those that are in the same field.

You may also have to resign yourself to staying with one employer in the earlier part of your career. The evidence from headhunters is that nobody outside will hire you to do a different job functionally, however good your track record, even in a related field. The implication of that is that those aiming at senior management will have to start making their smart career moves early on by making the decision to stay with the same employer at a time when most of their contemporaries are moving around.

CAREER MORAL   **You have to have a good deal of experience of line management, as compared to staff or consultancy roles, if you want to get to the top in business and industry; and in a large company environment that experience has to be gained in organizations of a similar kind.**

OLD MYTH   *Provided that you have the ability, success is just a matter of chance and luck.*

NEW REALITY   We would not deny that being in the right place at the right time has something to do with it. But you can improve your chances by making sure that the job you are doing has visibility. Headhunters look in places and at roles where achievement is demonstrable. From a career point of view, says Sir John Harvey-Jones,[9] 'public recognition is almost as important as financial reward'.

CAREER MORAL   **There are some roles in which visibility is easier to achieve than in others. It is better to be associated with the launch of a highly speculative new product or service than to be a brand manager of an established one – where the most you are likely to achieve is a tiny increase in market share.**

OLD MYTH *Success means getting to the top.*

NEW REALITY There is an increasing realization by individuals, especially among the younger, highly educated knowledge workers who have understood the career implications of the post-feudal workplace, that success is about self-development and self-actualization. An American psychologist, Dr Pamela Ennis, put it perfectly in a BBC interview:

> Let's understand that success does not necessarily mean being the president of a corporation or amassing millions of dollars. One has to take one's value system into consideration. Success is being the best you can be, according to your own definition of what's important to you.

CAREER MORAL **Success should be defined by the extent to which there is a match between your own abilities, expectations and values, not by your salary or position – unless, of course, that is how you yourself choose to define it.**

OLD MYTH *Your salary will rise steadily, year by year, if you just go on doing an adequate job and don't make any expensive mistakes.*

NEW REALITY Incremental annual pay rises still exist, but only in backward-looking organizations. Everywhere else, pay is now tied to corporate results and individual performance. The latter means, of course, that if the firm has a bad year, this part of the reward package will be affected. But there is a corrective element in the part that is paid for individual performance. That is generally tied to an annual performance review where targets for the next period are set and agreed.

In a well run organization, constructive mistakes are not penalized and may even be regarded as a positive sign – a willingness to take risks is an indication of leadership qualities. There is universal agreement with Harvey-Jones's view:

> Tolerance of mistakes cannot be infinite and mistakes vary a lot in kind. But mistakes which are made in an effort to change things, to introduce the new, to progress faster, deserve and

should receive high degrees of tolerance and sometimes even praise.

There is also a general view that 'asking for a raise' is not a good career move. If you have not received a raise which you think you deserve, the organization either does not value your contribution as highly as you do, or has failed to recognize it. In either case, the best plan is to think about making a move.

CAREER MORAL   **Organizations are becoming increasingly entrepreneurial. Entrepreneurs, almost by definition, are people who
take risks. Increasingly, financial rewards are the result of risks
that have been undertaken successfully. The big problem is for
people in staff roles, whose performance is more difficult to
measure in entrepreneurial terms.**

OLD MYTH   *Virtue and achievement will always be recognized in the end.*

NEW REALITY   Don't bank on it: prophets are never honoured in their own country, as the proverb tells us. Nicholson and West found that promotion, especially in small and medium-sized firms, was often made from the outside. That is one of the signs of weakening loyalties to which we referred in the last chapter. It does seem that the devil they don't know is better than the one they do. That may be because working alongside someone over a period of time is bound to show up some of their weaknesses. Another factor is that, in a climate of change, organizations look for people who can bring a new view of things and new contacts, and they tend to come from the outside. Companies are also sometimes attracted by the idea of bringing someone on board with experience and training that is already in place – so they won't have to pay for it.

    There is also an argument, in the light of the quote from Tim Bell 'the man who orchestrated the Conservative Party's election strategy when he was at Saatchi & Saatchi' in the previous chapter ('ultimately your only loyalty will be to yourself'), for regarding success and achievement as a personal asset. It is a realizable capital gain in individual career terms. In the post-feudal organiza-tion, that should accrue to the individual, rather than to the corporation. There must be many people who wish they had moved when their stock was high rather than when time and circumstance brought it back a few points.

CAREER MORAL **Waiting for dead men's shoes is usually a waste of time. They are seldom filled by an heir apparent, unless there is a definite undertaking to that end – and even then, the situation may be changed as a result of a merger or takeover.**

OLD MYTH *Lock you career on to a successful boss/mentor and rely on him or her to take you with them.*

NEW REALITY There are examples where this has been a smart career move, but more where it has not. The problems are as follows:

- He or she may be using your skills to mask his or her short-comings. Being indispensable to someone is flattering but may block your own career development. The crucial question is: Who is getting the credit when you make a contribution?
- Very high-profile bosses or mentors get all the publicity. Their adjutants get little or none. Who has ever heard of anyone at Amstrad other than Alan Sugar, its founder? Who has ever heard of anyone at Body Shop, other than Anita and Gordon Roddick? The question you have to ask yourself in career move terms, or the headhunter who may have approached you (in addition to the basic questions about the job itself, the money and so forth) is whether the high-profile person who is wooing you has a reputation for bringing on good people, whose own careers have benefited as a result. Some of the best training grounds for managers are to be found in companies that have a less than exciting image and do not in fact have a high-profile leader; organizations such as Procter & Gamble, NCR, Unilever and Mars.
- What will happen when the mentor moves on or falls out of favour? In a US company that one of us worked for in the 1960s, the company President's admittedly obnoxious mentee was out within days of his mentor's departure.
- Over-reliance on a male mentor has been identified as a problem for women because of its gossip potential.

The high-flyers interviewed by Charles Cox and Cary Cooper in a book of that name[10] did have mentors, but they built up a range of contacts rather than relying on a single mentor.

CAREER MORAL   **Only one person can really manage your career – you as its owner.**

OLD MYTH   *You've got to work hard to correct your weaknesses.*

NEW REALITY   This is often just a hangover from that part of the Protestant work ethic which says that if it hurts, it must be good for you.

A new reality is emerging out of the fact that people increasingly work on projects as teams of knowledge workers, pooling complementary skills. That means that you would be better off polishing your skills in the areas where you are already strong – which are usually those bits of the job you enjoy most anyway. The only other skill you really need is the ability to work with other people. But if you are a total duffer in a particular area – if you find financial matters unintelligible, or are poor at handling numbers, or expressing yourself in writing – you may have to give up some ambitions. For instance, there is very little chance of being accepted for an MBA course if you are innumerate: but that does not mean that you cannot get at least near the top, or otherwise have a satisfactory working life, in one of the many roles where numeracy of a high order is not essential.

CAREER MORAL   **You have to exercise judgement about where your efforts would be best directed, and learn to work in teams with other people who can complement you in areas where you are weaker.**

OLD MYTH   *You get what you see in the organization chart.*

NEW REALITY   We agree with an article in *The Times* a while back which said that relying on the organization chart to find your way around the power structure in most workplaces is rather like using the London Underground map to find your way at street level. The secret of the appeal of that immensely popular TV series, 'Yes Minister', to all sorts of people in all sorts of places very far removed from the British Civil Service, is that it tells what we know to be the truth about all organizations: that there is a reality of power and influence, based on contacts and knowledge of how you get things done, which supersedes what the chart tells you. Research on organizational politics shows that in order to get the ear and attention of decision-makers, you have to get past the 'gate-keepers'. These are usually secretaries and others who, although they scarcely figure on the organization chart, control access to those with decision-making powers. You also have to be aware of 'influencers'. These are people who have no ostensible power themselves, but on whose advice those who do have power depend.

CAREER MORAL   **Sir John Harvey-Jones sums it up in his book:**[11] **'unless you have worked out how things actually happen you have no chance of achieving anything at all'.**

OLD MYTH   *You have to be physically close to the people who hold the power to be visible.*

NEW REALITY   The trend towards decentralization and devolution in organizations means that what you actually do is what counts to achieve visibility, not your physical presence. In fact, corporate headquarters can be a dangerous place to be. That has often been where job cuts fall first, rather than in a company's operating units.

Devolution is another trend that is unlikely to be reversed, because information technology makes it less important for people to be physically present for many of the support roles that are carried out at corporate headquarters.

On the other hand, corporate headquarters remains the place where top management happens. If that is what you are aiming at, you have to make sure that what you do is visible to the people who are running the organization. More on that later.

CAREER MORAL   **At least in the early stages of your career, it is more important to be prepared to be mobile than to be close to the sources of power.**

OLD MYTH   *An internal promotion or upwards move is always a good thing.*

NEW REALITY   Organizations, as we have said in the last chapter, are changing their shape from hierarchical ladders to flat pyramids. Therefore results are not necessarily rewarded by promotion in its traditional sense. The immediate reward is more likely to come in the shape of a performance-related pay increase. But the positional reward may be a lateral career development move into another function, or being sent on a valuable course. Stephen Taylor of the London management consultancy, Kinsley Lord, talks of this as 'promotion to a particular job, rather than to a rank or grade'.

All of this is not to say that an actual promotion based, as Taylor says it should be, 'on talent rather than on the basis of Buggins's turn' should not be welcomed – provided that it fits in with a real understanding of yourself, your values and your real competencies. That is the subject with which we will deal in the next chapter.

CAREER MORAL   **Professor Peter Herriot, in *Recruitment in the nineties*[12] sees smart moves within organizations less as progress up a ladder 'which you climb up rung by rung – and then fall off' and more towards the idea of a series of agreements where both parties – employer and employee – agree on a set of mutual objectives. In the case of the individual these have to do with the fulfilment of career and personal goals. Not everyone, he says, necessarily wants promotion in the accepted sense. We go along with that view.**

OLD MYTH   *It's all over after you reach 50.*

NEW REALITY   The skills shortage, caused by steep demographic drop in many Western countries in the number of job entrants, is likely to change what we admit is a pretty entrenched set of attitudes towards the over-fifties; but it may not take the shape of further career paths within organizations. Indeed, organizations have to keep the upper levels clear in order to provide a view of the top for their high-flyers. The role of the over-fifties will probably be that of one-person self-employed consultants using their knowledge and experience to tackle specific assignments for a variety of clients, or as 'executive temps'.

We will probably have to get used to careers which are like those in the armed forces, where all but the most senior officers retire in their fifties. But that does not mean the end of their working lives – unless they want it to. The majority go on to a satisfying second career, in which the pension they are earning from their first one allows them a great deal of flexibility of choice in terms of function and the amount of work they choose to do. For many people, in fact, the so-called 'third age' is the time when they get to do what they always wanted to. But, as in the earlier career stages, you have to take account of your own strengths and weaknesses: as you get older these become, increasingly, physical ones.

CAREER MORAL   **After the late forties, start thinking about a 'third age' career, rather than your future within the organization.**

Notes

1 'Selling off the communist shop', The Economist, 11 February 1989.
2 T. Peters, Thriving on chaos (Pan, London, 1989).
3 C. Schnaars, Megamistakes (Free Press, New York, 1988).
4 J. Fairhead, Design for corporate culture (NEDO, London, 1987).
5 The Cookham Group, Headlines 2000: the world as we see it (Hay Management Consultants, London, 1988).
6 J. W. Hunt, S. Lees, J. J. Grumbar and P. D. Vivian, Acquisitions, the human factor (London Business School and Egon Zehnder International, London, 1987).
7 The Economist, 17 September 1988.
8 See A. Mumford, Handbook of management development, 2nd edn (1986) and Developing top managers (1988) (both published by Gower, Aldershot, Hants, UK).
9 Sir John Harvey-Jones, Making it happen (Collins, London, 1988).
10 C. Cox and C. Cooper, High flyers (Basil Blackwell, Oxford, 1988).
11 Harvey-Jones, Making it happen.
12 P. Herriot, Recruitment in the nineties (Institute of Personnel Management, London, 1989).

3

Personal Culture:
Careers as Autobiographies

In embracing notions such as corporate culture, corporate beliefs, missions, philosophies, value systems and so forth, people in management have shown their readiness to apply to the conduct of organizations lessons from other, so-called 'soft' disciplines such as sociology and anthropology. In fact one of the major shifts that has taken place in management since the early 1980s is the attention now being paid to aspects, particularly of organizational behaviour, which used to be dismissed as having little relevance to the hard, numerical, analytical business of managing an organization.

But there is one discipline that has largely missed out – psychoanalysis. John Dunn, the former London head of a firm of US consultants that specializes in occupational psychology, puts forward the interesting theory that this has something to do with the language and connotations of analysis. People still feel uncomfortable with Freudian ideas about complexes, the origins of sexual behaviour and so forth. And there is something definitely unmanagerial in the idea of undergoing psychoanalysis. To be frank, most managers would regard that as being but a step away from the funny farm.

Yet, when it comes to careers, analysis, in the sense that it is concerned with establishing a basis for self-knowledge, has an important role to play. For many of the 2300 managers surveyed by Nicholson and West, careers were 'improvised and haphazard. Many have unclear beginnings and no obvious endings; they just peter out'.

What makes the beginnings unclear is that they have no view of how the process of career management begins – with what is in themselves. Part of the reason for that is that, as we said in the first chapter, introspection and reflection are not qualities that have a particularly positive rating among managers, probably because they are not valued management qualities. Most managers would sympathize with the students at Manchester Business School who, when asked to take part in a process in which their peers would discuss frankly how realistic their aspirations were, mostly refused to do so. 'Ready, fire, aim' is the course recommended by Peters and Waterman in a chapter entitled 'The bias for action' in their hugely influential book In search of excellence,[1] but what is sauce for the corporate goose is not necessarily so for the individual career gander.

It is true that people who endlessly weigh up the options before they do anything will not make good managers, but there is a happy medium. To take the particular case of career moves, the financial and human costs of taking the purely action-oriented course of shooting for a job first and asking questions about it afterwards ('ready, fire, aim') are simply too great, for both the organization and the individual. However, it happens more often than it should, not only because of the cultural 'bias for action' in management but because finding your place on what one might call the multi-dimensional map of a career journey is very complicated. Here are some of the dimensions that need to be considered.

What you can do

In a sense what we are talking about here is a digest of your CV. What you can do is therefore largely a matter of record: tasks you have performed well and the skills, competencies, contacts and knowledge you applied to them or acquired in the course of doing them. However, it is important to look beyond the mere 'menu' aspect of what you have done and towards some under-lying pattern of events. Achievements are generally related to particular circumstances or settings and one should also look out for these.

It is the happy combination of talents and conditions suitable for exercising them that makes up the magic mixture of 'being in the right place at the right time' to which Cox and Cooper's high-flyers[2] attributed their success. For instance, Sir Michael Edwardes' combative style was undoubtedly right for seeing off the shop stewards at British Leyland in the 1970s. But his fortunes in subsequent years, when he failed to find a similar challenge, were mixed.

The importance of understanding the circumstances in which success is achieved is nicely illustrated in Lee Iacocca's autobiography.[3] When he was fired as President of Ford, the company had just made a profit of $1.8 bn. 'Mark my words, Henry,' he said as he stormed out, 'You may never see a billion eight again. And do you know why? Because you never knew how . . . we made it in the first place'.

What you could do

What you could do is to some extent a matter of opinion, your own estimate of your own abilities but also the opinion of others: comments on the lines of 'you're so good at this, that I wonder why you don't ask to be sent on a course, chair a meeting on the application of computers to a particular problem, handle the company's relations with the Press, or whatever.

It also has to do with unexploited potential. One of the people we interviewed provides a good example. A senior manager in a large company, he fell victim to a corporate upheaval and, despite a good track record, found it difficult to secure another job. However, in the course of being processed through an outplacement company, it emerged that he had never exploited his outstanding natural gift for languages. In the context of the single European market, that capacity, in addition to his experience and reputation, proved to be extremely attractive to employers and he was able to resume his career.

Picking up signs of this sort could give a new dimension to the career of anyone who had talents which were not being used but for which a demand is beginning to appear, either within an organization in which they are employed or outside it.

But you have to make sure they know what you could do. One of the leading consultancies engaged in applying information technology to human resource management says that firms often have no idea of the range of skills that people on their payroll have. Their personal record is confined to what they can do or have done in the organizational setting. It does not take account of what are often quite invaluable things which they know a lot about, possibly through outside interests and activities, and which could be translated into skills that they could apply immediately or with additional training to develop obvious aptitudes. With the worldwide shortage of skills the 'could do' element is likely to become of increasing interest and, indeed, a principal activity of this particular consultancy is to set up databases of internally available, but hitherto unrecorded, expertise.

It is not, however, something that exists in the abstract. It is only of use if it can be applied. So in looking at what you could do or at things about which you know a lot, you also have to consider whether your potential is tradeable. Where, to whom and when is it most likely to be useful? What do you need to do to make it so, if this is not immediately obvious?

What you want to do

What you want to do itself has two dimensions. In question and answer sessions about careers, with MBA students at Manchester Business School and at Harvard, many of the questions are focused on how to set about becoming chief executive of a company within the next 10-15 years. That is an understandable ambition in the circumstances, but it should only be part of the story. Someone setting themselves such a goal would not be likely to reach it, or at any rate would not be happy, and probably not successful in it, unless it fit the other dimension – their personal values, the things that are important to them.

There are, of course, people to whom functional goals are paramount because their personal values have to do with the things that accompany success: money, prestige, power and the trappings that go with them. But it is possible to have other values, or for these to emerge in the course of one's life. They might have to do with discovering the intellectual satisfaction gained from doing some jobs but not from others, with preferring to travel, or to work in a particular country or location, or simply finding that life or interests outside work are or have become a more important value than work itself.

What you want to do has to achieve a fit between internal values and external goals. One problem is that internal values can be changed by time and circumstances. Sir John Harvey-Jones started out as a regular officer in the Royal Navy. Rapidly promoted and highly qualified, he had a glittering career ahead of him when his young daughter developed polio. Because the Navy would not give him leave to spend more time with his family, he had to make a choice about his values. He decided that his family came first, so he abandoned his service career and made a fresh start in civilian life by joining ICI. You cannot anticipate outside circumstances, but it is easier to adjust to them if you start by knowing what your values are.

What you need to do

Career journeys can on occasion be directed by the need to make changes. You might need to get out of a situation where you are under threat or where your career is not providing the psychological or material rewards that you look for. Here again, it is important to be clear about your values, because, as we shall show in the next chapter, there are a number of ways – some obvious, some less so – in which needs can restrict the options that are open to you.

What might stop you

Apart from the constraints that we have touched on – lack of resources, family ties, and clashes between your internal values and your external goals – you might be stopped by personal shortcomings. The question then is: What can you do about them?

Some shortcomings are easier to overcome by training than

others. The ones that fall into this category are what a report produced by Ashridge Management College and the Foundation for Management Education characterizes as 'doing' skills.[4] Under this heading come specific technical/functional abilities, numeracy, literacy, the capacity to communicate and to think through and analyse problems, time management, and general managerial competencies in finance, marketing, project management and information technology.

However, the ability to put these skills into effect depends on another set of more shadowy, less specific 'people' skills: the ability to communicate, motivate, negotiate, delegate, work in a team and appraise. Some of these are teachable to a greater or lesser degree. But there is also another set of factors – attributes rather than skills – which have to do with personal qualities and characteristics, the absence of which might indeed form a constraint in certain directions. The report calls them 'being' factors. Typical being attributes include:

- being bright, quick-thinking and quick to get the point
- enthusiasm and energy
- presence
- ability to handle conflict and make decisions
- self-confidence
- strength of will
- commitment and determination
- flexibility and willingness to change
- creativity
- willingness to take responsibility and resilience in living with it
- initiative
- competitiveness
- sensitiveness to people and situations
- stamina
- commercial awareness
- judgement
- being personally 'organized'
- risk-taking
- ability to strike a balance between 'the big picture' and attention to necessary detail

These are qualities that you are largely blessed with or deprived of by virtue of those two rigid moulds, environment and heredity. One of the changes that has taken place in management thinking in recent years is the feeling that softer 'people' skills and 'being' attributes are as important as hard 'doing' competencies. As the Ashridge Report puts it, 'many of the characteristics that managers point to as desirable have as much to do with personality, attitudes and values as with skills and knowledge'.

Psychometric tests and predestination

There is a wide range of psychometric tests which have been designed to establish the presence or otherwise of 'doing', 'people' and 'being' attributes. There was a period in the 1960s and 1970s when such tests fell out of favour, in Britain at any rate, but in the 1980s testing made a considerable comeback because it became apparent that interviews by themselves had a rather poor record as a predictor of performance.

Certainly, in establishing 'doing' skills and potential there is a strong common-sense case to be made for testing. People who cannot deal with numerical concepts are unlikely to flourish in a role that calls for the interpretation of statistics, while those who have difficulty in unravelling a complex train of logic are unlikely to be suited to information technology environments, and so forth.

Tests of less specific skills and potential are more problematic. In his book on interviews,[5] John Courtis, a very intelligent commentator on recruitment matters, gives as an example a question in one of the standard personality tests which establishes levels of anxiety. Courtis makes the point that a low level of anxiety may be a very good thing in some circumstances, but it can also imply that the 'subject doesn't get anxious over things other reasonable people would get rightly anxious about, like meeting deadlines'.

Another influential critic of testing is the American writer William H. Whyte, whose book *The organisation man*[6] is one of the classics of management literature. He believes that a serious limitation of test techniques is that they produce questions framed in black and white terms, while real life is much more complex. Certainly, when we tried out the Cattell 16PF test, one of the industry standards, we were struck by the number of questions where the true answer, for instance to a choice between a variety of actions in a given situation, would have depended on the circumstances; but we were given to understand that neutral answers would result in an unfavourable score.

In *The organisation man*, there is an (only slightly) tongue-in-cheek section called 'How To Cheat On Personality Tests'. Whyte argued that in many cases the real object of personality tests was to find people who would clone the conformist behaviour which was preferred by the organization. Therefore, if you framed your answers to give the 'right' picture of yourself in their terms, you were likely to meet the criteria of the test. As a critical 1988 article in the *New Scientist*[7] put it, 'anyone with a moderate skill in acting can, for an hour, project an image of drive, confidence or whatever qualities a company may fancy it wants'.

There is something in such criticisms, but at the same time it is our opinion that the results of personality tests often do contain a preponderance of truth about what you are really like. So even if you fool the organization, you would be unwise to fool yourself. That leaves open the uncomfortable question, in relation both to being and doing skills, of the extent to which career paths are a matter of 'predestination'. This is a theological term, which means that you are either born as one of the elect or as one of the damned; and there really isn't anything that you can do about it.

The optimistic view is that, if you really want to, you can learn skills and change behaviour. That is certainly true up to a point, but it takes time. In real life, you may not have that option. A more likely form of action is to accept and be aware of the fact that you have some shortcomings, but to be equally aware of your strengths, to build on them and to work with people who have strengths that can complement yours. That is the recommendation offered by Sir Colin Marshall, the highly effective chief executive of British Airways. 'Nobody is equally good at everything, no matter how good they are in particular ways. Recognize your weaknesses and become a team leader of good people', is the advice he gave when we discussed this point with him.

There are good precedents for it. An extreme example used to occur in the British army, where it was accepted (in an unwritten way, of course) that young officers were less experienced and often less technically competent than senior NCOs who ranked below them. Faced with a problem to which they did not know the answer, but to which the NCO probably did, the three magic words were 'carry on, sergeant'. However, the understanding on which the success of that relationship depended was that the officer's 'being' aspects, lumped together under the heading of 'officer-like qualities', were in place; for instance, that he was able to make a decision, take responsibility for whatever happened under his command and set an example by his own physical and moral conduct.

At a higher level the most famous instance of someone who was effective in office despite what, by all accounts, were considerable 'doing' deficiencies, was President Reagan. His own technical competence in many aspects of his job was regarded by commentators as sometimes embarrassingly minimal; but he built on his consummate ability as a communicator, an essential core skill for a politician, and surrounded himself with able advisers. Here are some other ways of compensating for common weaknesses, either by good team-building or by avoiding situations which expose them:

Carelessness about detail   Have someone on your team who relishes it.

Poor ability to communicate verbally   Rely on good, well presented documentation. Follow the example of President Bush, a poor speaker, and keep speeches as short as possible.

Inability to delegate   Create good reporting systems that highlight only aspects that actually demand intervention. Go off on business trips that leave subordinates in charge, in whose work you might otherwise be tempted to interfere.

Culture and the Goering reaction

The mixture of goals, achievements, values, skills, and constraints which we have described adds up to what might be called a personal culture. It can vary in the course of a career through personal development and be revised in the light of experience but, broadly, your personal culture at any given point determines the direction of your career journey over the length of time in which it is practicable to make plans. We believe that is about the same period as that over which businesses can make plans, around five years.

However, whereas most managers accept the fact that there is such a thing as a 'corporate culture' – the way we do things around here – an individual's awareness of his or her personal culture often attracts the rather impatient reaction that is a sign of sensitivity rather than sense. It is, for instance, true that busy executives do not respond readily to academic researchers, but Charles Cox and Professor Cary Cooper found that less than half their sample of high-flyers were willing to complete a questionnaire about their personality and behaviour patterns. Similarly, occupational psychologists report that the vast majority of managers are reluctant to take psychometric tests unless they are facing a career crisis which highlights the need for self-assessment. As far as any attempt to dig into their personal culture and their psychological make-up is concerned, the reaction of managers is similar to that of Hermann Goering: 'Whenever I hear the word culture, I reach for my gun'.

Yet in career terms there is a relevant link between personal and organizational cultures: the way I do things and the way we/they do things. Both are an expression of values, beliefs, loyalties, attitudes, competencies, resources, a view of the market and of the lessons that have been learned from history.

In the case of organizations, these are what determine their behaviour. It is extremely difficult for them to do things that run counter to that, or to merge with other cultures if they are alien to them, or to live with people whose culture is markedly different. Terence Deal and Allen Kennedy, in their *Corporate cultures*,[8] illustrate this point in saying:

Bright young comers at GE could, for example, quickly fizzle out at Xerox – and not understand why. They'll be doing exactly what they did at GE – maybe even working harder at it – but their deliberate approach to issues large and small will be seen by insiders at Xerox as a sign that they 'lack smarts'.

They fail because, for individuals as for organizations, it is difficult to do things that run counter to the prevailing culture – in this case what you might term your personal culture. Yet that is what you would be called on to do when you link your career with a corporate culture which is alien to it.

People are aware of that when they talk of the good or bad 'vibes' they get from their impression of an organization, or when they talk about 'personal chemistry' between themselves and the people in it. Because of the suspicion with which introspection is regarded by many Western managers, the match or mismatch of personal and corporate cultures is expressed in these rather vague terms; and these signals are sometimes ignored by those who take a tough-minded 'doing' view of what leads to career success. Our view is that it is vital to be more consciously aware of your personal culture in order to make sense of the direction of your career as a whole. In doing so, you are only following the example of organizations who increasingly understand the need to audit their corporate cultures in order to give shape to their future.

Executive summary

As far as thinking about careers and career moves is concerned, the suggestion put forward for organizations by Peters and Waterman in In *search of excellence* also holds true for individuals:

> All that stuff you have been dismissing for so long as the intractable, irrational, intuitive . . . can be managed. Clearly, it has as much or more to do with the way things work (or don't) around your companies as the formal structures and strategies do.

We are, in this case, talking about applying the products of introspection and self-knowledge – a real understanding of where your strengths, weaknesses and limitations lie – to career moves and plans. There are two aspects here. One is concerned with *doing* skills – the technical competencies and achievements that you would list in a CV – and taking a realistic view about which are the ones that need improving, which are capable of being improved by action such as a career move, and which, quite frankly, are the ones you are stuck with.

For instance, a brilliantly successful newspaper editor of the 1960s and 1970s was famous for being an innovative and inspiring ideas man, but a notoriously chaotic administrator. However, the owners of the newspaper formed a highly successful alliance between him and a managing editor, an efficient, tactful former senior army officer. Both men were able to do what they were best at. But when the editor moved to another newspaper, his new managing editor was, like himself, a clever ideas man with a limited interest in detail. Instead of making up a team of complementary qualities, they were almost rivals. The results soon proved to be unhappy, both for them and their subordinates.

That provides the clue to the other, equally important matter of *being* characteristics. Being and doing exist in tandem and form a personal culture. You cannot get by without at least some colours from each palette. How far you get depends on how rich a choice you have. Even the great entrepreneurs, as the American writer Rosabeth Moss Kanter points out, are not in reality 'the sort of lone, egotistical individualist who can't work with anybody else'. They depend, in the end, on getting others to share their vision. In other words, technical skills are not enough on their own.

In the post-feudal organization, where people collaborate across broad layers of a pyramid rather than issuing and receiving orders, your 'being' characteristics are more important than ever. But that also means that you have to study the 'being' characteristics of the organization – its vision and corporate culture – and make sure that personal and corporate cultures are in alignment. That is a topic on which we will focus more clearly in a later chapter.

Notes

1 T. Peters and R. Waterman, In search of excellence (Harper & Row, New York, 1982).
2 C. Cox and C. Cooper, High flyers (Basil Blackwell, Oxford, 1988).
3 L. Iacocca, Iacocca, an autobiography (Bantam, New York, 1984).
4 K. Barham, J. Fraser and L. Heath, Management for the future (Ashridge Management College, Berkhamsted, Herts, UK, 1988).
5 J. Courtis, Interviews: skills and strategy (Institute of Personnel Management, London, 1988).
6 W. H. Whyte, The organisation man (Simon & Schuster, New York, 1956/ Penguin, London, 1960).
7 'Exercise that can prove a testing time for managers', New scientist, 29 September 1988.
8 T. Deal and A. Kennedy, Corporate cultures: the rites and rituals of corporate life (Penguin, London, 1988).

4

How Needs Can Tie You in Knots

One of the people who we interviewed as part of our research was the chief executive of a company he had started in the late 1960s. Let us call him Paul Cooper (not his real name). His firm has a turnover of several million pounds sterling. In the course of its expansion it acquired, almost by chance, in what was once a rather run-down part of London, freehold property which is now worth a great deal of money. Cooper Ltd itself has never been very profitable, although it has a good reputation in an important market niche and is involved in an industry which has attracted interest from a lot of major players. Mergers and takeovers for sums which have seemed out of all proportion to earnings have often been in the news.

Paul Cooper, who is now in his late fifties, is a phenomenally hard worker. His firm, which has had some dramatic ups and downs in its time, is the focus of all his energies. He talks and can think of little else, and there is a constant flow of problems; some minor, some periodically rather worrying. He pays himself quite modestly and enjoys very few of the trappings and benefits of owning a controlling share of an enterprise that is probably worth around £15–£20 m (that is the band of figures that has been mentioned by firms that want to take Cooper Ltd over).

A takeover would make Paul Cooper a wealthy man. Eventually his children, who have taken up other careers, would inherit a lot of money. But Paul will probably go on driving himself until he drops; or almost. The fact is that he does not want to sell, although it would make financial sense for him to do so, and although the bidders who make regular approaches to him would be glad to keep him on as chief executive. It might also be good for the firm, which has, on more than one occasion , been 'strapped for cash' at critical moments.

The reason for his apparently irrational stance is that his role as head of the company he founded fulfils his needs in a way that having several millions in the bank does not. His needs are for autonomy and, perhaps, power. Arguably, they will cause him to hang on too long, as many a CEO/founder has done before him. Perhaps this could be avoided if he recognized his needs and found a way of coming to terms with them.

Needs and career paths

In management literature the study of needs has been linked to the theme of motivation; in other words, to the physical or psychological rewards which people seek from their work in order to fulfil those needs. But this search also plays an important and sometimes unacknowledged role in the wider subject of career aspirations and in decisions connected with reaching them. It is, therefore, important to understand how needs arise and how they affect behaviour.

There are a number of theories about the development of human needs, but the one that is probably the best known, and of which most others are largely variations, was that put forward by Abraham Maslow.[1] Maslow divided needs into five main categories:

Physiological needs   These are concerned with basic requirements for survival and acceptable standards of comfort. In the job context they are concerned with earning enough money to live on, with decent working conditions, proper holidays and week-ends, and civilized working hours.

Security needs   These range from physical safety issues in and around the workplace to job security and some measure of predictability in the relationship between reward and perfor-mance. People who are worried about unpredictability in their environment, says Maslow, 'try frantically to organise and stabilise the world so that no unmanageable, unexpected or unfamiliar dangers will ever appear . . . they hedge themselves about with all sorts of ceremonials, rules and formulae so that very possible contingency may be provided for'. This is a good description of the obstructive behaviour of some middle managers when they feel under threat.

Social needs Maslow also describes these as 'love needs', although he stresses they have nothing to do with sex. Talking of the individual and using a gender-free masculine pronoun, he says: 'he will hunger for affectionate relations with people in general, for a place in his group and he will strive with great intensity to achieve this goal.' At work, social needs are expressed in the desire to belong to a team or a supportive group of like-minded people.

Esteem needs The need for esteem is the need for recognition and respect from fellow workers at every level. It is driven by the need to have feelings of self-worth, strength and confidence. The search for jobs with 'visibility' is one aspect of the search for esteem, but for many people job titles and status symbols are at least equally important. The latter are not, however, equally valuable in career terms, a point that is sometimes overlooked by seekers for esteem.

Self-actualization needs The need for self-actualization is what lies behind the desire to do work which provides job satisfaction. The content of such work has two main features: firstly, it carries responsibility and allows for a considerable degree of autonomy in the way it is carried out; secondly, it is something you are actually interested in doing and find helpful to the process of self-development. There is, or should be, a strong correlation between undertaking training and one's needs for self-actualization. Taking an MBA or an Open University degree are pure examples of the search for self-actualization in action.

Maslow's view was that needs are met through a logical, if unconscious, pattern of behaviours and actions. He saw them as a hierarchy in which physiological and security needs formed the lower tiers and the other needs formed the higher ones. A clear description of how needs develop and are fulfilled is given by the authors of *Working in organisations*:[2]

- Each lower-order need must be satisfied before the next higher-order need assumes dominance
- When an individual need becomes satisfied, it declines in importance and the need at the next level of the hierarchy increases in importance
- When the individual moves up to the highest-level need (self-actualization), satisfaction of this need increases in importance
- The sophistication and variety of needs increases as an individual's psychological development takes place

Those who have observed the behaviour of people in organizations have found that if their work does not satisfy their higher needs, they compensate by wanting more out of the lower ones – or by fulfilling their higher needs in outside activities. The manual worker, stuck in a boring, routine job, will go on strike for more money or collaborate with colleagues to hold down production levels by using restrictive practices and other 'anti-boss' devices.[3] People in lower-level administrative roles will complain about working conditions, although by contrast they will put up with awful ones if they are interested in what they are doing; in other words, if it meets the aspirations contained in their higher needs.

Similar patterns can be seen at every level in organizations. It explains why middle managers, concerned about job security, will anxiously guard their specialized knowledge and even surround themselves by physical barriers, such as a wall of filing cabinets, so that what they do cannot be overseen. It explains why some executives, feeling that they lack esteem, become obsessed with status or become involved in time-consuming activities outside the workplace, where their role gives them the recognition that is lacking in their work. It explains why the most active industry representatives on trade bodies are often recognized by people in the know as those who have not quite made it to the top in their own firms. One such man, who achieved national prominence in the 1960s as an industry spokesman, entered politics through this route and became a very senior government minister. But it was widely known that, much earlier, he had been passed over for promotion in his own firm, and that his involvement in the general issues of his industry had been a product of that fact. In her study of organizations from the inside, undertaken over a long period of time, Rosabeth Moss Kanter noted that 'When they are blocked from organisational recognition, people may substitute a variety of forms of "social recognition", finding ways to look good in the eyes of at least some other people'.[4]

All these are recognizable situations, but like a lot of temptingly neat theories about human behaviour, those of Maslow are only very broadly accurate. They do not explain, above all, why it is that for some people there are some needs which are clearly predominant irrespective of how well they are fulfilled, while they remain indifferent to the fact that other needs, seemingly at least equally important, remain unfulfilled. Some people, for instance, never lose their physiological or security needs. Money is absolutely predominant and all their career moves are determined by that. Others will have an overwhelming need for security: they will never take a job that involves a risk and will cling to an existing one in circumstances which most people would regard as humiliating and the clearest signal that it is time to move on. There are managers, generally politely described by journalists as 'abrasive', to whom socialization matters not a jot, but for whom money and achievement are absolutely paramount. On a different plane, there are people, especially among the younger age groups, to whom the self-actualization aspects of the job are all, and are certainly more important than money, security or the esteem of colleagues to whose values they are indifferent.

Another problem about following Maslow's hierarchy of needs too closely in marking out one's career moves is that they are not necessarily sequential in real life. That point was neatly, if incidentally, made in a classic advertisement for an insurance company. It is a strip cartoon sequence which begins with a young man who is quite indifferent to the fact that his job carries no pension, but who gradually works up to a crescendo of anxiety about it as he approaches retirement age. The importance of needs, in other words, is related to one's circumstances rather than to ticking off, in time sequence, the fulfilment of one need before moving on to the next one. For example, in the latter stages of one's career, security may be more important than self-actualization. The latter need might best be fulfilled by a community-interest role outside the workplace or by some form of self-development, such as taking an evening class or distance learning course.

For this reason, it is more realistic to go along with the argument of those who say that needs are a system, rather than a hierarchy. The most coherent explanation of this view in relation to careers is given by an American psychologist, David McClelland, who says that needs arise out of the mix of values and personality factors which we discussed in the last chapter as a 'personal culture'. They break down into three categories: the need for achievement, the need for affiliation and the need for power. In other words, we are variously motivated by the desire to meet objectives, by the need to belong to a group and by the need to influence and control other people. Again, in real life, it would be unusual for such motivations to appear in anything like a pure form – indeed, anyone who exhibited them in that way would be either a monster of ruthlessness or a cripple of dependency – but there is a preponderance of truth in this view that most people would recognize in themselves.

This means that one dimension of a job choice should be related to what you feel to be your system of needs. For instance, someone with a strong desire for achievement should aim for a job or an employer where performance is largely measured in those terms. Many US companies, for example, regard the public recognition of achievement as being a very important aspect of fulfilling needs and spurring motivation. The ultimate in this process is described in David Mercer's book on his years with IBM.[5] IBM has what it calls the 'hundred per cent club', membership of which is given each year to salespersons who reach or exceed their target:

> Salesmen are personally recognised for every conceivable virtue and achievement. It starts with the 'election' of the committee leading to that of the Club President. At my first US Club this latter part of the action was signalled by the President Elect being accompanied to the rostrum by a complete high

school marching band. As everyone is 'recognised' they run to the front, to the wild cheering of the members of their branch. Then the assembled masses sing IBM songs, without any trace of embarrassment and with great gusto.

People with a strong need for affiliation will find that their best work has been done as a member of a team, and might be advised to avoid jobs which call primarily for a solo performance, such as managing an overseas subsidiary. By contrast, those for whom control is important should look for a job or a working environment that is favourable to that style and avoid roles where it is not. A classic case of someone who did not observe this principle was that of a highly regarded but autocratic British chief executive who was headhunted for the top spot in a leading electronics company. His somewhat quarterdeck style turned out to be a disaster in a knowledge-based firm in which the leader was expected to be 'the first among equals', rather than a ruler laying down the law on each and every issue.

Like the human personality itself, though, these need traits only emerge, are recognized and develop in the course of time, as people realize that one need or other is an underlying theme to their choices and to the situation in which they flourish. Edgar Schein, an American professor who is widely regarded as one of the most perceptive commentators on the role of people in organizations, describes these themes as 'career anchors'. He suggests that they ought to play a strong role in career choices; and that ignoring that role is often what lies behind the reason why people fail to make the most of themselves in a career move. An excellent summary of these ideas was provided by Clare Joynes, then a student at Manchester Business School, in a dissertation on career development, sponsored by the executive search firm, Boyden International.[6]

The quest for stability

The quest for security and stability enters most people's lives at some point – usually one related to their circumstances. For example, a book publishing executive in his late fifties decided to leave South Africa with his wife and young children and come to England. Although highly qualified, he chose to take a safe but poorly paid job linked to a charity in the knowledge that it would provide job security until retirement. It turned out to be a more sensible course of action than that undertaken by his brother-in-law, who left at around the same time and went into another firm in a more high-powered role at more than twice the salary of the safe charity job. He soon fell foul of the egocentric owner of the company and then had the difficult task of beginning a fresh job search with a question mark, however unjustified, hanging over his recent career.

But there is another aspect to the search for stability. It concerns those for whom security and predictability overriding issues which consciously or otherwise guide their career decisions. Such people, says Schein, gravitate towards organizations that provide job tenure; which have a 'no redundancy' reputation, generous pension and retirement schemes and a reputation for stability.

In some cases this need for stability also has a geographical dimension. A friend of ours is a university administrator in a small northern town. Although extremely intelligent, technically competent and with transferable professional qualifications, he has never advanced very far in his career because of his unwillingness to uproot himself from the small community where he has spent almost his entire life. Public-sector organizations provide this kind of haven: as do large companies, in a different way. But there are sacrifices involved and it is important to be aware of them at the outset:

- Stability is not usually accompanied by high financial rewards.
- Those who are unwilling or unable to move with the play, psychologically or physically, are apt to find the game moving past them. As we stated in an earlier chapter, career moves, even within an organization, seem to be a prerequisite to advancement. IBM is a company with a high reputation for offering career development: the insider joke is that these initials stand for 'I've Been Moved'.

- Those who are unwilling to take career risks are marked out, as a matter of policy or otherwise, as typical middle-management material, no matter how technically competent they may be. Knowing that they will probably stay with the organization no matter what, they will be offered the less interesting assignments and less may be invested in training them for higher reaches of the organization, since they are suspected of being quite happy to remain with the roles with which they are familiar.

- The stability which is sought may be illusory. Even in the public sector, lifetime job tenure is becoming a thing of the past as it moves, like its private-sector counterparts, towards flat pyramids, fewer management levels and 'leaner, fitter' structures. In that process, it is the middle management seekers after security who have been most at risk; and because of their usually narrow range of skills and lack of experience of the wider job market, they have also been least well equipped to handle instability in their own lives.

But the picture is not all black, particularly if you start out with an awareness and acceptance of the fact that this anchor is important to you. As Clare Joynes concludes, after speaking to people in a variety of organizations:

> We should not assume that everyone wants to keep rising in the organisation. Many people, like the ones described here, have a feeling of having 'made it' even if they are not very high up in the organisation. If they have unused potential, they may prefer to find non-work and non-career activities to satisfy those unused portions of themselves. ... People are different and want different things from their careers.

The quest for autonomy

The person whose predominant career drive is a search for stability tends to like the rules and regulations that you find in such environments; and, as we observed earlier, they will try to

surround themselves with such mechanisms and even to manu-
facture more of them when they feel threatened. The course taken
by those whose needs are linked to autonomy and independence
is quite the opposite. Ultimately, such people are drawn towards
running their own business, but even in a corporate setting they
hate being bound by set procedures, regular hours, and even rules
about dress and behaviour. Their method of reaching objectives
and their view of how that should be done is like that of golfers
who say 'It's not how that counts, but how many'.

What we are describing here is an attitude that is found in firms
such as advertising agencies, design practices and in some high-
tech companies – but not, on the whole, in legal or accountancy
firms. It is one that is favoured by younger executives and arises
partly out of the freer lifestyles within which they have grown up
(we will deal with the relevance of childhood conditioning later in
this chapter) and partly out of the confidence, which some of their
older colleagues would describe as arrogance, which comes with
the possession of specialized knowledge.

A classic description of an environment in which autonomy
was the predominant corporate culture is given in John Sculley's
book, Odyssey.[7] Apple's executives, highly qualified at the most
exalted levels of electronics research and almost all independently
wealthy through stock options, took their cue from founder Steve
Jobs who wore frayed jeans and a cowboy shirt to work. When
Sculley arrived at Apple to take on the job of chief executive, he
was inundated with reports and memos from them – all too easy
in a firm where everyone had a computer on their desk. He then
tried to make a rule that he would not read a memo more than a
page long, but:

> It did not take much time to discover, though, that little is
> accomplished on the basis of an executive order at Apple. The
> chief executive could issue a directive here, yet no one would
> pay much attention to it. Independence was encouraged to the
> point where people felt they could make their own choices.

The growing importance of knowledge work and the increasing
status of the knowledge worker means that autonomy and

independence are becoming the predominant career style, but that also creates some problems. In his remarkably prophetic book, *The age of discontinuity*,[8] published in 1969, Peter Drucker pointed out that the knowledge worker of today is the successor not to the free professionals of the golden pre-war years, but to the employee of yesterday; and that sooner or later they come up against the reality that they are no more than 'the upgraded and well-paid successor to the skilled worker'. This, says Drucker, triggers off all sorts of tensions about 'stupid' authority figures.

It also creates problems for those moving from roles in which there is a lot of autonomy, which can be found even within organizations as niches in areas such as research and development, management information systems development and so forth, towards management itself. As Clare Joynes says:

> Management jobs have to be carefully analysed by the person who is autonomy anchored because they vary greatly in the amount and kind of autonomy they provide. Once one becomes a manager responsible for other people, for a budget, and for a certain outcome, this clearly limits one's degree of freedom. From one point of view, therefore, moving into management is the worst thing a strongly autonomy oriented person can do.

There are wide differences between companies as to the amount of autonomy they allow their people to have. At the giant conglomerate BTR, thought to be Britain's most profitable manufacturer, tight financial controls 'give the local management autonomy while subjecting it to rigorous financial scrutiny' - a case of not how but how many in action.[9] Clare Joynes found, though, that even within the same organization, management jobs differ in the amount of autonomy that they provide:

> Managers at the level of plant, division or a geographical region often report a high degree of autonomy. If they move into organisational headquarters, they often report a loss of autonomy. Some regional sales managers and some salesmen,

for example, refuse promotions into headquarters primarily because they are unwilling to give up the autonomy they enjoy.

There are people for whom the autonomy anchor is so strong that they are not really suited to organizational life at all. It is quite common to find successful entrepreneurs who describe themselves as 'unemployable'. Unfortunately, not everyone who gets upset when confronted by rules, red tape and established ways of doing things is cut out to be an entrepreneur. But in career terms, that kind of anchor would certainly suggest finding a role in which autonomous behaviour is rewarded – or at least not penalized. In the end, though, it is important to remember that you do also depend on being able to work with other people. That applies even to entrepreneurs if they want to stand any chance of success.

The quest for entrepreneurship

The entrepreneurship anchor is widely misunderstood. A lot of people think that what they would really like to do is to run their own business, and they are spurred on by stories of those who have made a success of it. But there are many more who either do not make it or whose ventures give them little more than a bare living.

One of the reasons why these misunderstandings occur is that there is a big difference between having a good product or a constant flow of bright ideas – or even having a lot of marketable skills – and being an entrepreneur. And an entrepreneur is not simply an enterprising person.

True entrepreneurs are a special, rather rare and not universally loveable breed. They start early, often at school or university or by running a business 'on the side' of their regular job. (To give just one example, Richard Branson, owner/founder of the Virgin leisure conglomerate was a successful magazine publisher while still at school and skipped higher education altogether.) They are single-minded to the point of obsessiveness about what they do, and if they have other interests these develop much later in life. They find nothing at all about business boring. They are natural risk-takers. They enjoy selling, and often start out as salesmen at the knocking-on-doors level. They are not averse to failure, and in fact many of them have at least one failure behind them before they achieve any degree of success.

Career consultants have found that many people who come to them with a desire to start their own business are either, in the words of one counsellor, 'scared job seekers' or those who think that running their own business will give them the security lacking these days in organizational settings. Nothing could be further from the truth.

The quest for specialization

Probably the most familiar career dilemma, both for organizations and for individuals, is that of the person who is good, even outstanding, at one job but who is a disaster on the next step up. A case in point was experienced by one of us when, as a general manager, he appointed as sales manager a young man who had been one of his firm's most able retail customers. But he proved unable to transfer the enthusiasm and commitment which made him such a success on the shop floor to the more ordered and systematic process which is additionally needed by a manager. Paperwork bored him, but he also hated spending nights away from home with his salesmen or on courses. Both his values and his competencies were at odds with the job. After a couple of unhappy and stressful years he went back into retailing, where he soon re-established himself as an exceptionally gifted performer in a clearly defined role.

Everyone who has ever worked in an organization could amplify such an example with those of good functional specialists who turned out to be hopeless managers, or even good managers of subsidiaries who could not handle the political relationships of a head office.

Edgar Schein would describe such persons as being 'anchored' in a particular function or competence and, to some extent, this is true of everyone; in the sense, at any rate, that we have particular talents or preferences related to values and skills to which we find ourselves gravitating in the course of our career.

This is a matter of degree. People who are very strongly competence-anchored may decide to remain within it, and for professionals such as architects or doctors a career ladder can be constructed around that: although even within the professions, narrow technical competence is now no longer quite enough to get to the top – or even to get by. For instance, what most architects like doing best is to design, but a review of the job market for building professionals produced in December 1988 by Incomes Data Services makes the point that 'Many employers are now looking for newly qualified architects ... who can run a project or manage a team'.

In organizations, it is even more difficult to choose to stay in one particular area, and not to be seduced by other possibilities, unless you make a conscious decision to do that almost from the outset. The problem with that course of action, however, is that the tug of career anchors is only sensed with experience of the kind of jobs and roles that one tends to enjoy and perform well in. Until such a pattern emerges – and even after that, in some unhappy cases – the natural tendency is for careers to follow fairly blindly wherever promotion prospects lead.

As we have seen, the route to general management runs either through a variety of functions – which is much the best way – or via a sudden transition from being a specialist to a generalist. In either case, though, people with strong career anchors may become victims of the Peter principle.[10] The rather thin book of that name simply makes the point that people are, in the end, promoted beyond their level of competence. They perform a particular task or set of tasks well, and are promoted as a reward each time they do this, but the sheer logic of events dictates that they will eventually get out of their depth.

That argument may well be true – but is it inevitable? In feudal organizations, in which managers have traditional goals about 'getting to the top' and a traditional reluctance to recognize their career anchors and admit them to themselves, it may well be. Post-feudal organizations are more ready to recognize that their executives may be best employed in 'sticking to the knitting' (as the authors of *In search of excellence* put it, in the context of a recommendation that companies should stick to what they are best at) and to create reward and career opportunities for them that run parallel to those of general management, except at the very top. For example, a 1989 report by Incomes Data Services[11] gives details of a number of companies that 'have introduced a "dual ladder" of career development, on which both the successful sales executive and the potential sales manager can thrive; in this way the sales executive who has no potential, or no wish, to be a manager can be rewarded with a higher salary grade'. However, pay is not related to sales performance alone. No career path can altogether avoid the interpersonal functions and analytical skills of management, but it can focus primarily on technical competencies.

The problem with competence/functional anchors, though, is that they can easily become obsolete unless you make a conscious effort to keep them up to date. Clare Joynes found that 'younger and more recently trained people often know more and can be hired at lower salaries, thus threatening the job security of the mid-life specialist'.[12]

The other problem is that those who are locked in to traditional assumptions about the course that their career ought to take are often unwilling to recognize that they may be happier and more successful in accepting the consequences of what, in their heart of hearts, they know to be their limitations.

The quest for a cause

For some people a career is related more strongly to their personal values than to such outcomes as material reward or stability. Again one has to see this in terms of a 'preponderance of truth' rather than an absolute, because attached to that quest for a cause would also be other career anchors such as functional competence.

People whose careers are anchored in the quest for a cause are likely to be attracted to what are called the 'helping professions', towards careers related directly or indirectly to various forms of public service. Under that heading come roles not immediately associated with what might be considered the 'softer' kinds of careers that are associated with causes: for instance, neither the police nor the armed forces are thought of in that way, yet a desire to serve the country or the community is often given as motive by those making their careers in them.

In organizations and companies, the immediate thought is that cause-orientated directions would probably point towards something to do with human resource management, but this is no longer quite the case. All organizations are now concerned with concepts of service and to a large extent these become a cause, as we can see from reading books such as *In search of excellence*.[13] Concepts such as Total Quality Management and Right First Time fall into this category, and have been suspected by some radical commentators as manipulating idealism to commercial ends.

Causes, incidentally, need not necessarily be related to social ends or even to customer service. The pursuit of knowledge for its own sake can be a cause and can outweigh commercial considerations in functions such as research and development. One of the reasons why the German computer giant Nixdorf ran into trouble in 1988, for instance, was because of its disproportionately high spending on pure research.

Certainly there can be a problem, in career terms, when a personal quest for a cause clashes with corporate objectives, shareholder pressures or guidelines that emerged with changes of circumstances. In the public sector this has been illustrated by cases such as that of the senior civil servant Clive Ponting, who leaked documents to the Press when he felt that an issue of personal value to him was at stake. Less dramatic, but perhaps equally agonizing, are the options faced by public-service professionals who find that their helping role is constricted by spending cuts; or by academics whose notion of 'value for money' is tied to scholarship rather than to class headcounts.

But even in service-oriented private-sector organizations there may be both commercial and human disjunctions between the organizations and individuals whose career anchors tend to be fastened to causes.

Fit for the future

How useful are these concepts of 'career anchors' in the hard, practical world of management training? For IBM (UK) – to give just one example – they are central to the whole concept of employee development. As the starting point of a programme it calls 'Fit For The Future' IBM asks employees 'to look inwards and so understand their strengths, values and options'. In an article in IBM's house journal, *Management Topics*,[14] two senior IBM trainers describe their programme as:

> ... like an archeological dig in which participants unearth shards, fragments of themselves which can gradually be assembled into a coherent pattern ... It is a driving force that underlines and connects the activities in a person's life in which there is a consciousness of being in harmony with his or her true self. ... The insight, when achieved ... can have a Eureka-like impact. In many cases it helps resolve confusion about motivation that may go back many years.

Raising the anchors

Some of the needs that act as career anchors are disabling or restraining factors if you have them to excess. For instance, a very strong need for security may inhibit you from making a move you know you ought to make, or may cause you to constantly look for the approval of others before you make a decision. At the other end of the scale an over-developed need for autonomy and independence is likely to make you a loner, or someone so un-disciplined that you cannot fit into any job for any length of time. So how do you get that way? And is there anything you can do about it? Understanding the reasons for your own behaviour will not necessarily enable you to change it absolutely, but it is at least a step on the way to making some adjustments. Training is, after all, not a matter of absolutes but of degrees of improvement.

An explanation of the roots of needs that affect behaviour, and which managers from all sectors find illuminating, is offered by the British psychologist Tony Lake. In line with IBM's theme that motivation can 'go back many years', Lake believes that adult needs are triggered by early childhood conditioning: the child controls its behaviour in the interests of the adults upon whom its existence depends. The years from birth to about nine crucially affect later behaviour because almost the entire growth of the brain takes place during that period. Although learning is a continuous process, it is during this phase that it happens most quickly.

In its early years the child is totally dependent upon adults for its physical and psychological resources, but adults, in order to survive the stresses and strains of child-rearing, have to have a policy about the resources they are prepared to allocate and how they do this. Lake describes it as a 'power struggle' and says that child-rearing uses three main groups of controls: squashing, ignoring and rescuing.

The child who is squashed may itself become a squasher in adult life: at best a leader, at worst a domineering autocrat. The other option is to attempt to win approval from the psychological successors of a 'squashing' parent. As an adult, this person will set him or herself very high standards, but will lack confidence about ever reaching them. He or she will look for a parental figure in workplace relationships and will back away from leadership roles.

The 'ignored' child will go on playing by itself in adult life, and will be creative, imaginative and inventive. But at the other end of the scale, ignored children can turn into attention-seekers, exhibitionists, and irritating clowns at inappropriate moments.

The supportive 'rescue' relationship is the healthiest one, and certainly the one that is now most strongly approved in middle-class child-rearing practice. Lake believes that it is reproduced in adult life by devotion to causes and by altruistic rather than material ends. Certainly its prevalence in child-rearing in the post-war era may explain attitudes of concern about such matters in younger age groups, and their relative indifference, in some cases, to conventional ideas about career progress. On the adverse side, though, it can cause people to try to reproduce situations in which they expect someone to come to their rescue; for instance, to dramatize trivial dilemmas or to sulk until they get their way.

Alternatively, they can overplay the role of rescuers. For example, one manager on a course that we observed had been promoted from a human resource function in which he had successfully played a 'rescuer' role to a line management job. He was having great difficulty in adapting to his new role because he tended to help his subordinates, when he should have been giving them guidelines and letting them get on with the work – a benevolent mix of 'squashing' and 'ignoring'.

As in all theories about behaviour, Lake over-simplifies many issues, but the fact that managers on Lake's courses recognize their validity suggest that the theory offers 'a preponderance of truth' about the patterns that people can observe in their own behaviour. It also links in with the ideas of people such as Maslow, McClelland and Schein, because it is equally probable that there is a relationship between, say, an excessive need for security and childhood conditioning, or between a lack of interpersonal skills and having parents who lack sensitivity in dealing with children. To accept the enduring influence of these experiences is probably the best way of coping with them as we go along, making our own way and career in the world. In the words of an article in the *Harvard Business Review* by American psychologist Harry Levinson,[15] 'Armed with an understanding of his ego ideal [another way of describing what Schein calls a career anchor] and working style, the manager is now ready to weigh options more wisely'.

Executive summary

What drives people to make career decisions about moving on or staying? The direct answer is that such decisions are triggered by the need, conscious or otherwise, to acquire some of the career management tools which we mentioned in the first chapter: money, training and development, or visibility. There may also be other reasons, such as simple restlessness, boredom, a desire to move to another part of the country or wanting a different life-style. Equally, the decision to stay in a particular job, sometimes in circumstances which puzzle bystanders – and occasionally the jobholder him- or herself – is made because it satisfies their needs.

The classic case is that of people who have a very strong need for security and will stay in a dead-end job for that reason.

Understanding the nature of the needs that drive career decisions is an important part of the process of acquiring self-knowledge, to which we referred in the previous chapter. It not only explains past actions and helps to provide the 'clear beginnings' which Nicholson and West found that most careers lack, but it also throws some light on whether a career move is more or less likely to satisfy the need that occasioned it. For instance, if you have a very strong need for affiliation, a move to a role which will isolate you may not be a good one.

The career implication of all this is that people should consider the extent to which their present job fulfils their current physiological, social, security, esteem and self-actualizing needs. If it fails to do that to a significant extent, the reason may be a mismatch between their current roles and the precise nature of the career anchors they tend to seek. For example, a quest for self-actualization may be linked to entrepreneurship, not to the form of self-actualization which their current role provides; or they may have stronger need for socialization than that provided by an autonomous role and seek, more than they should, to avoid unpopular but necessary decisions in order to be liked.

These dilemmas are not easily resolved. But being aware that they exist is at least the first step to overcoming them, either by job changes or by seeking appropriate training. In fact, the best organizations are beginning to recognize that truly effective training is an individual rather than a mass-produced process.

Notes

1 A. Maslow, *Motivation and personality*, 2nd edn (Harper & Row, New York, 1970).
2 A. Kakabadse, L. Ludlow and S. Vinnicombe, *Working in organisations* (Penguin, London, 1988).
3 V. H. Vroom and E. L. Deci, *Management and motivation* (Penguin, London, 1970), pp. 218ff.
4 R. M. Kanter, *Men and women of the corporation* (Basic Books, New York, 1979).

5 D. Mercer, IBM: how the world's most successful organisation is managed (Kogan Page, London, 1987).

6 C. Joynes, Executive career development research project (1988, unpublished).

7 J. Sculley, Odyssey: Pepsi to Apple (Harper & Row, New York, 1987).

8 P. Drucker, The age of discontinuity (Heinemann, London/Harper & Row, New York, 1969).

9 Sunday Times, 5 March 1989.

10 L. J. Peter and R. Hull, The Peter principle (William Morrow, New York, 1969).

11 Incomes Data Services, Pay and bonuses in sales (Research File 11, Incomes Data Services, London, 1989).

12 Joynes, Executive career development research project.

13 T. Peters and R. Waterman, In search of excellence (Harper & Row, New York, 1982).

14 Tom Jennings and Sheila MacLeod, in IBM (UK) house magazine, Management Topics, issue 34, February 1989.

15 H. Levinson, 'A second career: the possible dream', Harvard Business Review, May–June 1983.

5

Avoiding the Dorian Gray Factor: Time, Personal Development and Careers

Literary quality alone does not account for the enduring impact of Oscar Wilde's celebrated but now largely unread fable, *The picture of Dorian Gray*. Its universality has to do with its power as a metaphor of the gradual changes that occur in people in the course of their lifetime development. They are invisible in the image you see each morning in the mirror. They are only brought into the open by some crisis which forces you to face some inner truth about yourself. As with Dorian Gray, it then emerges as a portrait that you know is there but have kept hidden away.

In career moves, what one might call the 'Dorian Gray factor' is important for a number of reasons. One, which we will develop in later chapters, is that it is on the whole advisable to choose organizational settings that are appropriate to the point you have reached in your lifespan development. For instance, there are perils in moving into a young, fast-moving organization at a stage in your life when, for physical as well as psychological reasons, your values may be focused on stability and order. Another reason is that career problems are often triggered by a feeling that there is some kind of dysfunction between the stage your life has reached and the demands, or lack of them, of the job you are doing. The enormous worldwide success – and continuing sale – of Gail Sheehy's book, *Passages* (tellingly subtitled, 'The predictable crises of adult life')[1] shows that it struck a theme, the truth of which was widely recognized. What we would like to do here is to relate that theme more strongly to career terms.

The mid-life crisis: confusing signs at the crossroads

The argument of *Passages* and of the more academic research by the psychologist Daniel Levinson on which it is largely based[2] is that the whole of life is a continuing series of crises, and that adult development is a life-long process of coping with them and learning from them. However, the one which everyone recognizes, and which has had most publicity, is the mid-life crisis.

A good account of how it affects one's career is given in John Sculley's book, *Odyssey*[3] – indeed, it is the starting point of his subtitle's journey: *Pepsi to Apple*. Sculley was in his mid-thirties, and as the $500 000 a year President of Pepsi had already reached what most people would regard as the pinnacle of their career, with status symbols to match. He writes:

> My suite, a 30 by 20 foot room, was comparable in size to the White House Oval Office. A Persian rug covered the hardwood floors, antiques and fine paintings decorated the space. Nine windows looked out over the sculpture garden and a small private garden below it. I had a private bathroom, an entry foyer where my executive assistant Nanette, and my secretary sat, and another private office where I kept my computers.

When a headhunter approached him to ask whether he would be interested in moving over to Apple Computers as chief executive, he was not interested; well, not *very* interested. He was sufficiently intrigued to go to California for a meeting with the legendary Steve Jobs, who had started the firm in the bedroom and garage of his parents' house a mere six years previously, and had propelled it into the Fortune 500 top US companies in that almost incredibly short time.

Sculley's memory of that encounter was one of enormous excitement at meeting people who were 'turned on' by aspects of business that did not greatly interest Pepsi. He had reached a stage in life and in his career when his strengths as a person and as a manager had begun to emerge quite clearly. His meetings with Apple had crystallized a conviction that what he most enjoyed in life 'wasn't running large administrative organisations. The things I enjoyed most were working with small teams, creating ideas and turning them into products or market opportunities'.

His energies as President of Pepsi, the job to which he had been appointed after successfully turning round the company's loss-making international operations, were poured into something called The Pepsi Challenge. This profoundly futile event was a nationwide blind tasting in competition with Coca Cola. Sculley, incidentally, treats it with a great seriousness that is quite revealing about the qualities that you need for success at the highest level ('The challenge seemed to symbolise the ideas of the country's new mood', he writes – a sentiment which reminds one of what founder Ray Kroc said of the success of MacDonalds: 'We just take hamburgers more seriously than anyone else'.)

Nevertheless, Sculley could not have been entirely convinced that it filled a gap in his life. After he had turned Apple's offers down several times, Steve Jobs hit him with a classic mid-life question: 'Do you want to spend the rest of your life selling sugared water, or do you want a chance to change the world?' This was another kind of challenge altogether, and one to which there could only be one answer.

It is rare to find a fabulous opportunity waiting to be taken up at this point in your life, but the feeling that there ought to be more to it than is on view in one's present situation is very common. The mid-thirties to early forties are years in which the top managers of the next decade are beginning to emerge, or are already in position; but they may have come to realize the personal sacrifices that involves, which in turn raises the question of whether or not the job is intrinsically worth it.

This is particularly an issue with women. The late thirties are the last chance to start a family, and an increasing number of women executives now have their first child at this time. Although an increasing number of organizations are offering career breaks to employee–mothers, it is still unclear what effect this will have on their careers, says Lindsay Miller, managing director of the Economist Intelligence Unit. She became a mother for the first time at 38. The biological urge to have children, which she thinks is innate in women, took precedence over her career in her scale of mid-life values, and although she feels that she can handle both, she admits that it is a gamble. The question facing organizations with women executives who are also mothers is whether or not they can provide a context which will enable them to be both in equal measure. Where this is not the case, women will have to make a mid-life choice that is probably final.

This is not a choice that affects only first-time mothers. The costs of success and ambition are heavy, even purely in terms of hours worked. All of Cox and Cooper's high-flyers, for instance, worked a 10–11 hour day and also took work home. That requires making some sort of choice between career and family.

It is a choice that is felt less acutely by men than by women with older children who have to be ferried to and from activities, whose homework has to be supervised and who simply require the physical presence of their parents between starting school and the later teenage years. Culturally, it is expected that the mother will play that role. Part of the mid-life crisis for women executives, they say, is their feeling of guilt if they do not take it up. Nannies, servants and the paraphernalia of what has been called 'the million dollar mother' (the total cost of her salary and that of the support system she needs to enable her to earn it) may not turn out to be a substitute for a gender role that is probably as old as the presence of life on Earth.

The crisis of choice between home and work is perhaps not so dramatic for men, but it is just as real. At this time, writes occupational psychologist Paul Thorne, 'he feels uncomfortable that he has not given his children all that a good father should. He has no time or energy left for interests outside work.'[4] That feeling is fuelled if there is doubt whether what you are devoting most of your waking life to is actually worth doing – the sugared water question.

It is particularly acute because, as Harry Levinson points out,[5] 'by their middle or late thirties, managers usually know how far their careers will take them'. The signs are partly external – the high-flyers will by then have observably taken off. Headhunters say that the age of 35 is the benchmark. You have to be either within sighting distance of a main board appointment or close to being chief executive of a significant subsidiary by then – or you are not going to get above the marzipan layer. That brings those in the latter group face to face with their limitations and the credibility gaps between early illusions, the career hopes which are consciously or unconsciously attached to them, and the realities of what has been achieved so far.

That gap is often due to lack of opportunity, or the right kind of opportunity, rather than to any individual shortcomings. The situation is neatly summed up in Levinson's *Harvard Business Review* article:[6]

> Some people feel they are no longer running for advancement, that their talents and skills are not being fully used and some that they have outgrown their jobs, companies or disciplines. Others, feeling blocked by being in the wrong company, industry or position, are bored. Some are in over their heads, while others had merely drifted into their jobs, or chosen directions prematurely. One of a combination of these feelings can make a person hate to go to work in the morning.

Research carried out both in Britain and the USA shows that the mid-life years are the ones during which the job mobility graph turns sharply upwards, before falling equally sharply as people approach the late forties. It is by no means always due to the negative feelings that Levinson describes: as in Sculley's case, clearly defined strengths and preferences will also have emerged as signposts of future career directions.

It is increasingly common for these to give rise to thoughts about self-employment, for a number of possible reasons:

- Because the corporate world, by its nature, does not seem to offer solutions to frustrated ambitions, or
- Because there is a feeling which might be summed up in a phrase such as 'Why am I working flat out to create wealth and assets for someone else, when I could be doing it for myself?', or
- Because of a view which might be summed up in the words 'The only job security I am ever going to have is that which I create for myself by being my own boss,' or

- Because of a perception, which is probably correct, that the late thirties to early forties is the last chance one will have to build up a sizeable business of one's own.

Self-employment can be successfully undertaken at any age, and there is an increasing number of instances of retired people taking this route. But the sheer physical energy required to run a business, and the time it takes to get it going, limits the options almost as surely as the way the biological time clock runs out for child-bearing.

We will deal more fully with the pros and cons of this option in chapter 11, but at this point we want to re-emphasize what we said in the previous chapter about the extent to which the entrepreneurial anchor is misunderstood, perhaps because of the publicity that is constantly given to the enterprise culture. What is less publicized is that only about half the new enterprises that are started ever succeed on anything more than subsistence terms, although we have also found that a lot of people believe that being their own master more than makes up for a gain in uncertainty and a drop in income. In other words, a surprising number of people get to a point in mid-life at which they find that their autonomy anchor is stronger, and their security anchor weaker, than they had supposed.

It is very important, though, to get career moves, whatever their nature, right at this stage in life. As a survey conducted by the international recruitment firm MSL showed, employer prejudices make it increasingly difficult for managers to get back into an employee role once they get past their mid forties. For this reason, MSL suggested, one should be prepared to face the fact that the music may stop in mid-career: the chair you are sitting in may be the one you will occupy for the rest of your life. That is a chastening thought, which in itself can be the cause of mid-career crisis.

That crisis is often bound up with personal crises as well, particularly marital problems. It is the age at which people get itchy feet, in both their personal and career spheres. But, warns a leading headhunter, 'the first move is often a wrong one, particularly if it's due to psychological and personal pressures. A switch is not something to be undertaken without careful thought about objects or the real reason for wanting to make a move'.[7]

The roaring twenties: all systems go

It is no coincidence that a great many people formulate radical views in their late teens and keep them through their twenties. Psychologists believe that an important part of the process of self-development, in the literal sense of developing one's own identity, is to reject the values of parents. By extension that means rejecting those of the older generation (or even half generation) in general.

Creatively, that can be very valuable: some of the most significant scientific discoveries have been made by people questioning assumptions at a very early stage in their careers. But in organizations the questioning process that is an essential preliminary to finding new answers can be a prime source of conflict. The classic gut reaction of their older members is to dismiss younger colleagues as know-it-alls and to wait eagerly for them to make mistakes. That, we suspect, is at least part of the reason why some British managers have a poor opinion of newly qualified MBAs. 'They are over-priced, highly mobile and a pain to share an office with', according to an attitude survey conducted by *Business* magazine.[8] On the other hand, the classic approach of aggressive Young Turks is to attack established ways of doing things, for some of which at least there may be a perfectly sound, or inescapable, reason.

A good example of this was experienced by one of us while working as the general manager of the subsidiary of a major but troubled company in the 1960s. Headhunters brought in a young chief executive with an impressive track record in another business sector. Within a few weeks he had produced a brilliantly argued diagnosis of all the things that were wrong with that company, which he presented to its senior managers. After a few respectful preliminaries some of them pointed out that the problems that he had identified were largely to do with the fact that the company was itself in a declining industry, suffering from too many low-margin products competing with each other in a narrow, inelastic market. He then impatiently sacked most of the executives in the company who had drawn attention to this fundamental problem – probably the very ones who might have come up with workable solutions under what was undoubtedly a dynamic leader – and replaced them with high-priced young talent from other businesses. They brought along ideas which had worked in their previous environments, but which were mostly totally inappropriate to their new setting. The results, needless to say, were disastrous and the chief executive himself departed after two or three traumatic years for all concerned.

A lot of promising careers were temporarily stopped in their tracks by this episode, but the young managers involved learned a useful lesson, which is to be very careful about stepping into situations where what you want to do is going to be very difficult to achieve. That may be, as in this case, because the traditions of the industry or the market it is in offer limited scope: for example, many headhunters take the view that, at least until recently, the UK construction sector fell into this category, because the firms in it tendered on price rather than on quality. That had the effect of perpetually depressing the salaries on offer and hence the quality of the people attracted to the business. Or it may be that the culture of the organization offers the wrong alignment between your values and needs at that particular stage in your life, and those of the organization. A brash, aggressive young manager, eager to make his or her mark, might find life difficult in a very staid, conservative environment; just as, at a later stage of development, they might be out of place in a young, hard-driven fast-moving consumer goods (FMCG) setting.

There is sometimes a correcting factor in the shape of a mentor, an influential older manager who will champion your ideas, shield you from the envious attentions of the enemies that young managers almost inevitably make, point out the pitfalls and sometimes even cover up for your mistakes. Mentoring has been much written about as a good role for senior managers to take up as part of a succession planning policy but, according to Professor Alan Mumford,[9] it is as yet not widely practised.

In general, therefore, young managers are left to learn from experience, and the frequency of job moves in early career stages seems to be a conscious or unconscious recognition of the importance of that. The sociologist Professor Ray Pahl sums up this phase as follows:[10]

This is the period of testing, switching, experimenting and gaining experience. This period may be used to gain experience, gain accurate knowledge of the job situation in appropriate limited areas, make contacts, get further formal qualifications; thus career considerations may be allowed to override all others.

There is, however, a crucial question buried in this statement: What are the 'appropriate limited areas' in which one needs to obtain experience? Headhunters talking to students at Harvard Business School make a number of points that indicate that if you look at the long-term career implications, the choices may not be as wide as even the most highly qualified entrants to the job market might think:

- It is increasingly difficult, as you grow older, to move from consultancy and financial services firms to line management, although in the short term the most tempting financial inducements usually come from the former. Apart from other considerations, those same financial rewards may make you too expensive when you want to move out into line management.
- It is difficult to move from small firms to larger ones; and it becomes more so as you grow older. The way each of them operates is too different. At least that is the perception at present: if companies take on the 'gazelle' role envisaged by Tom Peters (small and fast-moving in order to survive), small-company experience will become the flavour of the decade in the 1990s.
- At present many of the most valuable training and learning opportunities are to be found in large companies that rate low on sex appeal. At Harvard Business School, students are advised to join such firms in the first instance, because they can afford the mistakes which, in the view of ICI's Sir John Harvey-Jones and many other highly respected managers, are an essential part of the learning process.
- Doing what you are best at will probably produce the best performance and hence the highest visibility: but beware of being typecast as an expert, unless you are so incandescently brilliant that this can form a career in itself.

In career terms, the chastening thought that emerges is this: young managers in their twenties probably devote about as much thought to their career pattern as they do to their pension. Yet some of the decisions and moves that they make then can have a long-term impact, which generally surfaces at mid-life crisis time.

Thirtysomething: the make-or-break years

The next phase is one of transition, where you realize that things are more complicated than you thought in your first impatient years. You discover that in work, as well as other aspects of your life, the best way of getting to your objective may not be to head down a straight line between your start and your goal. That is where you begin to become aware of office politics, and that perhaps there is a good reason for some of the practices and procedures that you questioned earlier. The experiences of Mike Hall (not his real name) are a case in point:

I joined a big, fast growing retail group as a graduate trainee in the early 80s. It wasn't my first choice but it turned out to be a good move because I really found myself enjoying it all. I was picked out as a high flyer, managing one of its major stores after only about five years, and really given a surprising amount of autonomy in the way I did the job. Then I was brought into head office as a business development manager – I was still only in my twenties and at that point I'd gone beyond most of my contemporaries in my career.

I got married at that point and our first child came along fairly soon. Financial commitments were pretty heavy – nothing I couldn't handle in relation to my total package – but I'd bought an early Victorian house in an inner suburb and the out-goings were a bit larger than we'd anticipated.

I occasionally looked at job ads because at head office I could see that the management wasn't all that strong. In fact it was a bit chaotic in some ways, but the company was doing well in spite of that because of the retail boom in the mid eighties. I realised that the autonomy I'd had as a store manager was due to the fact that there wasn't much direction around the top. The chief executive was an autocrat, who ran things very much by the seat of his pants, though very effectively I must say. But the business had gone beyond the point where that was enough and some of the people around him weren't so hot. I did think of moving on, but I didn't think I could justify the risk – and I was earning a big salary and I had a lot of money coming to me in share options.

Around this time you might remember there was a lot of publicity being given to franchising as a means of expansion. Essentially it means that you licence someone to run your outlets, train them to operate independently and then take a royalty on their sales or a mark-up on the goods you supply them with. Instead of being a branch manager, to a large extent they're running their own businesses. That's how Benetton and Body Shop work and I thought that, given our fairly loose controls, it made a lot of sense for us.

I pushed for it very hard as a matter of fact, commissioned some quite expensive consultancy and feasibility studies, but there was a lot of opposition. The chief executive hated the idea because he didn't like not having absolute control, but never quite said no, because he could see that something had to be done to keep up the momentum of expansion. But politically I didn't catch on to the kind of gut feeling he had about it. And I suppose some of the older managers weren't too anxious to warn me – they didn't really mind the prospect of a high flyer coming off his perch.

Anyway, eventually there were some well-publicised examples of franchises coming unstuck, and the board killed the idea. I still think it would make a lot of sense for us, or at least for some of our activities because we're not doing very well as we were. I think it's worth a try, but can I get any support? Well, it's a dead issue as far as this company is concerned, but I realise that I should have been less abrasive about putting it forward. A lot of the people here, from the boss down, took it as a criticism of the way they were running the business.

It hasn't done my career here much good – doubts about my

judgement, I suspect – but what should I do now? A few chums and I are thinking about a management buy-out and I think we have a fair chance of getting a deal, but of course it means a big drop in my income just at the time when school fees are beginning to loom. The other option is to change jobs – our shares have dropped back, so the loss of options isn't such a big factor – but the fact that I've been with the company since I started won't count in my favour. Most of my contemporaries have got wider experience. I'll probably take a chance on the buy-out. I've talked this over a lot with my wife and she's willing to go along with whatever it takes to make it happen.

Mike Hall's story illustrates several points about careers at thirtysomething. He has been brought face to face with both external and internal constraints: office politics on the one hand and, on the other, his own lack of political skills in getting support for a solution that might well be the correct one.

There is some evidence that the thirtysomething barrier is even more marked for women. Certainly there is universal agreement that women have to be better than men to reach the same level. At this point in their career they hit what has been identified earlier as 'the glass ceiling effect' – invisible barriers which prevent women from rising to the top in organizations where the power brokers are predominantly male. At this point many of them decide to drop out, having found that the choice between family and relationships and a career is a zero-sum game – heads they lose, tails they can't win.

Christina Loomas, a senior manager with the Post Office, reporting her experiences on a study tour of the USA organized by Ashridge Management College, found the situation all too familiar:[11]

On the one hand they must prove themselves more competent than their male colleagues if they are to overcome the suspicions and prejudices of the men who make the decisions. . . . On the other they must avoid becoming too masculine in terms of forthrightness, competitiveness and aggression, as these qualities are often perceived as threatening by male colleagues and bosses when manifested by a woman.

The strategies that she recommends are worth quoting in full, because (with due adaptations) they also apply to men at the critical thirtysomething stage when, like Mike Hall, they have come to understand something of the environment within which their career has to develop:

> The key to success seems to be to develop political sensitivity: to learn to manipulate the system to one's advantage within a very narrow band of accepted female behaviour, and to package and sell oneself in a way acceptable to predominantly male decision makers. This means selecting carefully the areas where one chooses to fight.

The other option is to start your own business, and a considerable number of women have been spectacularly successful. Thirtysomething is the best time to do it because for most people that is when experience, vigour and motivation seem to converge on their highest common factor.

The other point about this phase is that you have begun to recognize your career anchors and your management style. In Mike Hall's case, security has emerged strongly – possibly too strongly, but his wife is a compensating factor. If it were otherwise, family circumstances might be an added strain when he finally does decide to take the plunge.

As far as his style is concerned, what emerges is that he is stronger as an ideas man than as implementer. He had many of the right management 'doing' skills, as his rapid rise in the company showed. But he lacked the 'being' characteristics to get them accepted. That means that the composition of the buy-out team of which he may be a part will be vital to its success.

45–55 is a dangerous age

By the mid to late forties those who are going to get to the top in their organizations will either have made it or will be within striking distance. For the rest, the options to move around in search of better opportunities will gradually become more limited, as we pointed out in the earlier section on the mid-life crisis. Nevertheless, Nicholson and West's study of managerial job change[12] shows an increase in mobility at this time: the same thing happens in the USA, according to an article in the *Harvard Business Review*.[13]

The reason is partly, in the words of that article, 'one final attempt to migrate to yet another company', but at least equally often now such moves are involuntary. At the level of the middle manager who is not going to get above the marzipan layer, most of what is now sometimes being euphemistically called 'downsizing' takes place. This is either to create room for the promotion of younger managers on the way up; or because information technology has indeed lessened or dismantled altogether the role of many middle management jobs in which managers who were not going to get much further could be parked; or because of a culture clash between an older manager and an organization with new ideas. That is what happened to Dennis Hart (not his real name) when at 52 he found himself being outplaced by the firm whose business he had built up:

When I took over the European operations of the American pharmaceutical firm who'd headhunted me at 38, there wasn't much there except a small import and distribution facility. Fourteen years later we had a major manufacturing plant in the south of England, a $75 m turnover and 100 employees; highly profitable and really my work and that of the team I'd built up. So what happens? Our American parent gets taken over and a bunch of, I must say, pretty unsophisticated chaps from the Midwest come to look us over. On the basis of a consultant's report, which incidentally they didn't tell me they were commissioning, they say we've got to close down here and relocate in Holland because most of our growth is going to come from the Continent and communications with our European customers are better there. Absolute rubbish with the Channel Tunnel being built, but they insisted. I stood my ground, expecting that my record here would uphold me against them, but the new chief executive in the States didn't support me. I was just a name to him, anyway. So who's looking for a 52 year old research chemist? After what I've been through in the last year, I feel I've had it with being a manager.

Dr Hart will almost certainly get another job, although probably not as a research chemist. One of the big problems at this phase of one's life is a kind of 'de-skilling' effect of management. Doing other things takes you away from your original competencies and, in technical and scientific areas, qualifications gained even a decade previously are likely to be of limited direct value.

Indirectly on the other hand, his scientific background could be immensely valuable, as was shown by the example of a venture capital company that hired a redundant scientist of Dr Hart's calibre to help them evaluate the science- and technology-based schemes that were put to them.

But in accepting his next offer, he will be well advised to look at the management style and culture of his next employer because, as the MSL survey we quoted earlier points out, this may well be his last chance to find a role as an employee (self-employment is something else, but of that more later). We shall say more about culture later too, but when joining a company at this age Dr Hart should think about which of the classifications suggested by Brian Bartlett in an article in *Management Today* it falls into:[14]

Exploitative   Big financial incentives, but lots of pressure and a limited amount of time to make the grade.

Laissez-faire   There are no problems, because no one is prepared to recognize that they exist. It could mean the good life for those who don't want anything too demanding; but it might not last.

Integrative   Try to manage change by sharing objectives and building up teams of people with complementary skills.

Dr Hart has one satisfying consolation: his previous company will almost certainly regret losing him. 'Older managers', say Nicholson and West, 'have higher levels of loyalty, commitment and job involvement'. As we remarked in the first chapter, these are qualities which at the moment are not highly valued. But the backlash is coming, as employers increasingly realize that a young, footloose, knowledge-oriented workforce, committed only to its own interests and perhaps those of its peer group, leaves a hole in the middle of where the accumulated wisdom of the organization used to be. 'Companies become reserves of accumulated experience, reservoirs of knowledge, inexhaustible mines of information', says Alfredo Ambrosetti, head of the Italian management consultancy group that bears his name. Being able to tap into these sources is also a part of 'making it happen', a phrase that Sir John Harvey-Jones has introduced into the management vocabulary. Reading his book of that title, it is clear that part of his success was due to the fact that, unusually these days, he was a lifetime employee of the company of which he became head.

After 55: grey power

Is there career life after 55? We have to say that a lot of recruiters in Western countries do not think so. In fact, the 1989 survey conducted by the human resource consultants MSL, to which we have previously referred, showed that where an age was specified in job advertisements, 90 per cent placed an upper limit of as low as 40.

That attitude tends to bring about a self-fulfilling prophecy. Older managers, other than those who have made it to the top, tend to be low on confidence and self-esteem because they are perceived as being burned out and used up. In fact, this is part of another set of old myths that has to be confronted with new views.

OLD MYTH   *From the mid-fifties on, people are less able to assimilate new skills.*

NEW VIEW   Research by Peter Naylor, chairman of the Institute of Personnel Management's equal opportunities group (who himself completed a PhD at 50 plus) shows that people vary at every age in this respect. It is a matter of ability as much as age. However, according to psychologist Bill Acker, at any given level of ability, older workers do experience a decline in their capacity to handle operations that require both speed and accuracy. As another occupational psychologist put it to us, 'they couldn't trade in front of an electronic screen in the City'. But that is itself a very narrowly specialized skill. Bill Acker says that 'mental efficiency does decline with age, but not sufficiently to matter much'.[15]

Another telling point about learning capacities as you grow older is made by occupational psychologist John Dunn, until recently the London head of Rohrer Hibler Replogle, one of the world's leading consultancies in this field. He says that older people still learn, but they learn differently and in some respects more effectively. They relate new information to experience and make patterns that they can recognize – but they are less good at learning new things from scratch.

CAREER MORAL   **If you are faced with having to learn new skills after 50, pick areas where you can build on knowledge that you already have. A classic case is that of information technology. You are probably too old to learn state-of-the-art technical skills, but at almost any age you can learn enough about IT to make the all-important connection between that and business strategy. This gives you an edge over technologically adept, but commercially inexperienced whizz-kids.**

OLD MYTH   *The skills required by senior managers have changed so much that the over-fifties cannot handle them.*

NEW VIEW   A survey conducted by Market and Opinion Research (MORI) for the health insurance firm BUPA indicated that at these levels the most important qualities were the ability to delegate, to manage others, to make good decisions, to identify the essentials and not to panic when things go wrong. These are the very qualities that good over-fifties possess.

The one new skill they need to acquire is a rather modest level of computer literacy and keyboard manipulation. The computer's ability to hold and recall data actually compensates for one real disability that comes with ageing – the loss of short-term memory.

CAREER MORAL   **There is general agreement that a basic familiarity with information technology is the essential that is common to almost all jobs.**

OLD MYTH   *Older managers do not fit in with a younger workforce.*

NEW VIEW   There is some truth in this if one is talking about young industries, especially if they have grown up around a youth culture, although even then there are exceptions. For instance, one might think that no one over about 35 would fit into the environment of computer games, yet the deputy managing director of Virgin Mastertronic – the Virgin company that specializes in this field – is 56; and that in a firm where the average age of employees is 25–28. That supports the evidence given to a Select Committee of the House of Commons[16] by the Institute of Personnel Management, which indicated there was no support for the notion of a generation clash. On the contrary, sociologists say that as judgemental attitudes towards the younger age groups among the older ones have declined, the generation gap has actually narrowed.

The big problem that does come with ageing is that of health, and to some extent stamina. That is why starting up a business at a later age is something that has to be tackled with caution, although the opportunities for consultancy, part-time work and non-executive directorships are improving with the change in the nature of the workforce, as we shall show in chapter 11.

Even in starting up new enterprises there are exceptions to the rule. Lord Thomson of Fleet was Mr Roy Thomson, a relatively small-time owner of a chain of provincial Canadian newspapers when, at the age of 60 plus, he bought The Scotsman, sold and leased back its valuable property assets at a sum which gave him the newspaper for nothing, saw the potential of the Scottish TV franchise which he secured on the strength of owning the newspaper and coined the immortal phrase that it was a 'licence to print money', then went on to bid for North Sea oil rights, which yielded a fortune that made even his previous acquisitions seem like small beer.

On a more everyday scale, a close relative of one of the authors, having had one successful business career, began another equally successful one at 60 in a totally different field. He then sold out at a huge profit at 69 and began looking for yet another new opportunity. 'Retirement is for the elderly', as a 70-year-old entrepreneur told The Times not long ago.

CAREER MORAL   After 50 or so, you still have to be careful to pick the right career setting and the right corporate culture. Older managers are less suitable for high-pressure roles and corporate environments; for instance, those where performance is measured by quick results. One can make a comparison with sport. Plenty of older people compete successfully in marathons, but not in sprints because these call for a kind of strength that you do lose as part of the ageing process. The secret of good late career moves is to pick a setting in which wisdom and experience are properly used and valued, as is the case with some non-Western companies; or where it is an asset, as is the case with training and mentoring roles.

Executive summary

Although different stages of lifetime development do not have distinct beginnings and endings they do have preponderant themes. In this chapter we have allocated these to a number of chronological periods in the lifespan of individuals.

During the early years of a career, roughly up to the late twenties, a combination of high physical energy, currency of qualifications, a low level of material commitment – and hence a high level of scope for mobility – maximizes freedom of choice. These are also the years when people change jobs most frequently.

There are, however, two enemies of promise to be aware of. One is a potential clash between high personal energy, coupled with inexperience, and the inertia, real or apparent, of some organizational settings. The career lesson was summed up by one talented, but tempestuous young manager: 'If you want to rock the boat, don't go out to sea with a load of old age pensioners'. The other is that some of that early freedom is illusory in relation to later career events. Certain early choices seem fateful for those with senior management ambitions; in particular, choices between large and small companies and between consultancy and line management.

In the early thirties the options narrow as one begins to become exposed to physical constraints in the shape of material commitments – a house, a family and so forth. For women, there may have to be a choice between a career and a conventional marriage. For example, whose career interests are to be paramount in a relationship where one partner is offered a job which requires relocation?

The early thirties is also the time when substantive promotions begin and the high-flyers pull away from the pack. By that time you are aware – or should be – of the outlines of your management style, your work preferences and your strengths and weaknesses at work. These should now be signposts in making career moves.

By around 35 those who are going to make it into senior management in larger organizations are in place. For them this raises the question of whether it is actually worth making the sacrifices that are going to be involved. For the rest, the issue is that of coming to terms with the fact that they will probably have to stay around the marzipan layer. Good moves focus on work preferences: 'If you are going to have to like what you get, you may as well get what you like', is how one 42-year-old manager put it. That applies to the organizational setting as much as to the nature of the work. This is another period of considerable career movement because many jobs specify, openly or otherwise, an upper age limit of around 45–50. For a good many people, reaching that age band is likely to be the last chance to make a move as employees.

The other career option is to go out on your own. Once again material circumstances – fewer financial and family constraints – coupled with experience open up the range of choices.

After 50, the nature of executive work stresses the role of wisdom rather than energy, although at the very top you have to have both in equal measure; in fact, high energy levels throughout their lifespan development is one of the few characteristics that many very successful people have in common. Those below the top should be in settings in which wisdom and experience are valued. Wise movers identify such cultures before making a career move. Existing attitudes to older workers are the best indication. Are they being used productively and intelligently to create a corporate blend between wisdom and energy?

The core theme of this chapter is as follows. Throughout a career, smart moves are those that successfully identify appropriate organizational settings and career choices and align them with lifetime development. These depend, in turn, on being aware of what is happening, physically and emotionally, at the various stages of individual development.

Notes

1 G. Sheehy, *Passages* (E. P. Dutton, New York, 1976).

2 D. Levinson, *The seasons of a man's life* (Knopf, New York, 1978).

3 J. Sculley, *Odyssey: Pepsi to Apple* (Harper & Row, New York, 1987).

4 P. Thorne, 'Executive behaviour: In today's changing world, is there life after 40?', *International Management*, February 1988.

5 H. Levinson, 'A second career: the possible dream', *Harvard Business Review*, May–June 1983.

6 Ibid.

7 G. Golzen, *Jobs in a jobless world, where they are and how to get them* (Muller, London, 1983).

8 P. Benjamin, 'Europe discovers the golden passport', *Business*, February 1987.

9 A. Mumford, *Developing top managers* (Gower, Aldershot, Hants, UK, 1988).

10 J. and R. Pahl, *Managers and their wives* (Penguin, London, 1971).

11 Ashridge Management College, *Women in management* (Ashridge Management College, Berkhamsted, Herts, UK, 1988).

12 N. Nicholson and M. West, *Managerial job change: men and women in transition* (Cambridge University Press, 1988).

13 J. Veiga, 'Do managers on the move get anywhere?', *Harvard Business Review*, March–April 1981.

14 B. Bartlett, 'The bypassed manager', *Management Today*, June 1987.

15 W. Acker, 'What happens to management skills after 40?', paper presented at BUPA Conference, 'Over the hill at 40?', 1988.

16 'The employment patterns of the over 50s', Minutes of Evidence to the Select Committee of the House of Commons on Employment, 8 June 1988 (HMSO, London).

6

The Right Stuff

'When I started out, I wanted to be like Richard Rogers or James Stirling',[1] said a highly successful middle-aged architect to whom we spoke, mentioning two of the biggest names among his professional contemporaries: 'But I realised I just wasn't as original a designer as they were, so eventually I just settled for doing the kind of work I was good at and enjoyed doing'.

The fruits of that decision could be seen in his lifestyle; a beautiful house in one of the best parts of London, a long and congenial marriage and a very solid professional reputation. He treats the fact that his career has been sound, rather than brilliant, with relaxed good humour; probably because he has defined success in his own terms, rather than on those of the external conventions which say success is all about 'getting to the top'.

Architects, surgeons, barristers – in fact, professionals in general – find it relatively easy to establish how much of the right stuff they have, and where their shortcomings lie. They can define realistic career goals quite early. That is because much of what they do is a solo performance and they can measure its success by the roar of the (figurative) crowd.

It is far more difficult for managers because much of their work focuses around their relationships with others. Their success depends as much on the *being* attributes that we described in chapter 3, as it does on the *doing* skills that we also listed there. These networks of dependencies on the judgement of peers and bosses also make them much more vulnerable to what are still traditional, externally determined, ladder-climbing expectations of what success is, rather than on providing their own script.

One of the problems now faced by people in organizations is that there are fewer rungs on that ladder. The growth in information technology, as many commentators have pointed out, has removed the need for most of them. Sir Colin Marshall, chief executive of British Airways, told students at Manchester Business School in 1989:

> It is perfectly possible now to postulate companies with only three levels of management: that which runs the tasks, that which both plans the operational policies and acquires the resources and that which deals with the strategies and the people policies involved.

Getting to the top – or even getting close – in the traditional sense is getting tougher, and the journey was never easy anyway. Nor can you relax when you finally get there. Virtually all the high-flyers interviewed by Cox and Cooper in their book of that name[2] testified to the long hours they worked and how little time it left them to lead any kind of private life.

Dr Pamela Ennis, an American psychologist interviewed on BBC Radio 4 raised another point: 'I've always found that the person who rises to the top has to have a certain ruthlessness', she said, in reply to her interviewer's suggestion that 'people who get to the top in business are not particularly nice'.

There is evidence that some of the requirements and characteristics that put younger managers in particular off about jobs at the top are changing. According to an exhaustive international survey of the attributes which chief executives now look for in their successors, produced by the headhunting firm, Korn Ferry,[3] the initials CEO (chief executive officer) also stand for creative, enthusiastic and open-minded. They are replacing older requirements such as tough (i.e. ruthless), conservative (i.e. stuffy), dignified (i.e. pompous) and patient (i.e. reluctant to rock the boat). But they still list a long menu of attributes which are needed to make it to the top.

Assuming that this is your aim, you have to ask yourself: Do I have enough of the right stuff? Without it, the sacrifices of time and wider personal interests that the arduous road to the top entails may never be worthwhile. Professor Hans Eysenck, the psychologist, is one of a number of researchers who have concluded that managerial leaders are born, not made: 80 per cent of an individual's personality attributes, he says, are genetically driven – only 20 per cent can be learned.[4]

Managers and leaders

The single quality that is most generally identified as being necessary for those who want to get to the top is that of 'leadership'. But what is it that differentiates leaders from managers? And is there any real difference between them? The American management writer, Warren Bennis, has provided a definition of the distinction which is widely accepted. Managers, he says, do right things. Leaders do things right. In other words, managers are concerned with efficiently marshalling the physical resources of the organization. Leaders have the gift of inspiring people with a vision of the direction in which the organization, or even just their bit of the organization, is going.

In reality management needs a bit of both. Even so-called charismatic leaders, who involve themselves very little in the day-to-day business of management, need good commercial judgement and the ability to build teams if they are to succeed. Hitler, for instance, is often picked out by managers as having been a good leader, leaving out the ethics of his regime. But he failed because he substituted hunches for work and because he lacked judgement.

Rather than talk about leaders and managers, one should therefore talk about managerial leaders. And although their characteristics are potentially almost endless, because success (as we shall go on to show later in this chapter) is also related to circumstances, there are some themes which run in common. Predicting success is a matter of looking at yourself and your life and career paths to date, and seeing how many of them have emerged in your case.

High parental expectations British psychologist Tony Milne has found that a noticeable proportion of chief executives who appear in

Who's Who were elder sons. The assumption is that they were the children of whom the highest expectations were held. We found that a very large number of the successful managers who we interviewed cited the influence of their mother as being decisive. 'She always expected me to be a leader', said one chief executive, who was also fairly typical in being able to trace a consistent pattern of experiences in leadership from his early schooldays on. With women, it may be the father's role that is decisive. That certainly seems to have been the case with Mrs Thatcher: her father looms large when she talks of her formative childhood years.

Early experiences of leadership   'The best predictor of job applicants' future behaviour is what they have done in the past', writes another psychologist, Dr Jim Mackay, in a paper on biodata, an assessment technique which is gaining ground amongst recruitment professionals. The idea behind it is that key talents and aptitudes emerge early and point the way to future performance. 'Did you ever build a model airplane that flew?' is reported to have been a better predictor of success in flight training than the whole battery of US Air Force pilot tests. Similarly, many managerial leaders had previously been elected by their peers or superiors to leadership positions in sport and other activities.

Such experiences reinforce that quality of 'supreme confidence' that Antony Jay (the co-author of 'Yes, Minister') attributes to 'winners' in his earlier bestseller, *Management and Machiavelli*.[5]

Ability to have – and communicate – clear objectives   On the day when Field Marshal Montgomery arrived in the Western Desert to take over the demoralized Eighth Army in 1942, he called all his staff together and told them what changes he was going to make immediately, what he expected of his subordinates and what he intended to do about the enemy. 'A spirit of hope, at any rate clarity was born that evening', he writes in his memoirs.

The clarity was also a product of his ability to express himself in metaphors everyone could understand – another sign of managerial leadership ability. He talked of 'hitting Rommel for six' (the equivalent, in cricket, of a home run) and then followed his plan with absolute and highly visible consistency and determination.

Ability to take risks that come off   That is connected with doing skills such as the ability to analyse a situation and calculate the odds for success. It also fits in with confidence and with being able to pick the right issues on which to take a stand. Nelson exhibited this to perfection when he turned a blind eye to the signal from a superior officer ordering him to withdraw at the Battle of Copenhagen. He not only took a risk – he took it on an issue for which it was worth taking a risk.

However, Cox and Cooper make the point that risk-taking is not to be confused with gambling. Most of their high-flyers[6] saw themselves as only 'moderate risk-takers' – presumably because of the care they first took to calculate the odds.

Decisiveness   Managerial leaders are not always right; but they make decisions – and are not afraid about making unpopular ones.

Autonomy   The last point ties up with an observation that Warren Bennis has made about the numerous business leaders he has interviewed. They do not need the approval of others. 'It should not really matter how many people like leaders', he says. But the desire to be liked and the open or hidden fear of doing things that make you disliked is one of the major barriers to leadership. The young high-flying chief executive of the subsidiary of a major company, to whom we spoke, admitted that he had problems with 'being firm with people' – especially with those around his own age. For example, he had found it very hard to sack a secretary whom he liked personally but who was incompetent. Eventually he was able to handle such problems by making up his mind about how far he was prepared to let people 'bend things' and standing firm on issues and standards that mattered.

Psychological and physical stamina   All the leaders we interviewed emphasized not only the importance of making decisions, but of sticking with them. That came with an ability to put up with a lot of stress and with being physically able to work long hours.

Most managerial leaders are what others would call workaholics. We even heard of one chief executive, head of one of Britain's largest companies, who flew off to Japan on Christmas

Eve because Tokyo was the only business centre in the industrialized world that did not close down over Christmas. A doctor in the City whose speciality is executive health told us that it is not uncommon for business leaders to fly to New York on Concorde, return the same afternoon to attend dinners in London and be back at their desks at 8 am the next day. A high proportion of the respondents to a survey conducted among 40 major UK companies by the Institute of Manpower Studies concluded that energy and drive were among the key attributes for managerial leaders.

Ability to pick people   In terms of the 'career anchors' described in chapter 4, managerial leaders have a relatively low need for affiliation. But they are not loners. Rather, they are good at team building and delegating. Having done that, they then take care not to get involved in detail or to interfere any more than is necessary in the way the people they have picked do their jobs. They are extremely skilful at spotting winners among their subordinates, giving them clear directions and objectives, and letting them get on with it – even sometimes at the expense of letting them make 'learning' mistakes.

Ability to recognize their own strengths and weaknesses   The chief executive of one very large company made the surprising admission that he was 'not at all numerate' and found it difficult to analyse financial data. In spite of that, he had risen steadily in a career path that had included working directly under one of the toughest bosses in Britain for several years. 'I've been lucky in getting the support of very bright people who can help me in these things', he told us: 'And I've always made sure that I can get someone like that on my team. I don't bullshit them either – I'm quite frank about the areas on which I need help, and as far as possible I specify what I need to know. I think they respect my strengths in other fields and that in most of the areas that matter, I'm a pretty good all-rounder'.

The chief executive of another firm, talking of his early experiences as a leader in school sports teams, put it another way. He said that he had been 'a good captain, in spite of the fact that he was not necessarily the best sportsman in the team'. What he had learned from this was the realization that his *being* strengths – in this case his all-round ability as a team captain – outweighed his doing shortcomings as a player. Indeed, the fact that he was not a threat to any of the star performers was a positive advantage.

Finding the right setting

If there are these sets of characteristics that are common to managerial leaders, why is it that individually they are often more successful in some corporate settings than in others? It is not just a question of the Peter Principle which, to repeat what we said earlier, states that in hierarchical organizations the tendency is for people to keep on being promoted until they pass the level of their competence; rather in the same way as high-jumpers reach a bar height that they can no longer clear.

The Peter Principle can certainly be a factor, but it is also not uncommon for the reverse effect to take place. There are some notable instances of managerial leaders who have come from nowhere, or even from a previous failure.

- Tim Waterstone, who built up a successful chain of bookshops in Britain through the 1980s, started his venture after being fired as chief executive of the US subsidiary of a big British company.
- Andreas Whittam Smith had achieved little of much note until he became the extremely successful editor of The Independent. Indeed, in some respects his career gives the lie to the predictability of biodata. His school and university career had, on his account, been undistinguished, and in the army he had been told that he was unfit to lead men. It was not until he 'fell into freelance journalism' that he discovered where his talents lay.[7]
- Arthur Walsh seemed set to play out time as 'the small and retiring'[8] head of Marconi, one of the many subsidiaries of GEC, when he was picked out by Lord Keith, the then chairman of STC, to become chief executive of that company. They formed a highly successful turnround team and Walsh went on to succeed Keith as chairman. Keith had spotted that underneath a diffident exterior, Walsh is 'as tough as they come when it comes to squeezing performance out of a given asset'.

- It is an open secret among recruitment intermediaries that the head of one extremely large, well run and profitable PLC arrived at it by the unusual route of outplacement by his previous employer.

The libel laws in the UK being what they are, examples of top managers who have failed are not often written up, but there is no lack of examples of managerial leaders – including one or two who were knighted for their services to industry – who were either not able to sustain their performance or to replicate it in another setting.

One answer to this puzzle is suggested by two American consultants, Paul Hersey and Ken Blanchard, who are quoted in *Working in organisations*.[9] They say that, in essence, a managerial leader is faced with two predominating options for making things happen. He or she can either tell people what to do and give them clear instructions about how the task should be carried out (task behaviour); or the leader can operate through discussion and consensus (relationship behaviour). They go on to say:

A leader will be effective when he matches his style to his own requirements, those of his subordinates and the task itself in the context of the situation or environment. The individual manager needs to work out which approach to use, which combination of task and relationship behaviour is appropriate, depending on the circumstances which prevail.

What this means in practical terms is that in troubled organizations or groups the emphasis of leadership style should be on task behaviour. The point is illustrated by Lee Iacocca, in talking about his early days at Chrysler:[10]

I watched in amazement as executives with coffee cups in their hands kept opening the door and walking right through the President's office. Right away I knew that the place was in a state of anarchy. Chrysler needed a dose of order and discipline – and quick.

However, with organizations or units in which people are motivated, and conscious of their roles and responsibilities, relationship behaviour is more appropriate. An excellent description of a relationship style of leadership is given in Sir John Harvey-Jones's bestseller, *Making it happen*. He writes how one of his first acts, on becoming chairman, was to change the seating arrangements in the boardroom because he wanted the directors to act as a 'band of brothers'.

The problem, as the authors of *Working in organisations* point out, is that we all have a preferred style of management, which is related to our *doing* attributes – which is why it is unwise to take business autobiographies as recipes for leadership. There are some managerial leaders who, frankly, are at their most effective as authoritarians, and others who are more effective in more open, participative settings. The secret of smart leadership moves is to pick organizations that allow one to operate in a style which is personally appropriate – but to keep an eye on changes which might call for a different pattern of leadership behaviour. One of the problems the agents of change can run into is that they are sometimes slow to see the implications of what they themselves have brought about. There are smart moves out of a job, as well as into one.

Executive summary

The new, flat-pyramid shape of organizations, with only a few layers of command, is making it harder to move up a conventional career ladder. Thus, career choices are boiling down to accepting what are, in a conventional sense, 'lesser' roles in which success is determined by your own agenda, or a set of standards agreed with the organization. But if you are ambitious to get to the top – and to be honest, a lot of managers do entertain such ambitions, at least up to their early thirties – how do you know that your hard work, and the personal sacrifices that are entailed, will be rewarded?

Some characteristics and attributes of managerial leaders do emerge from various studies that have been made of them:

- high parental expectations
- early experience of leadership
- ability to have and communicate clear objectives
- ability to know one's own strengths and weaknesses
- ability to judge and take risks
- ability to pick people
- autonomy
- decisiveness
- energy

But even having all or most of these qualities does not guarantee success as a managerial leader. There are also personal styles of leadership. Very broadly, these fall into two types: authoritarian or democratic. Making smart moves is a question of picking organizational settings and situations that align with one's personal style – and also being aware of the need either to adapt that style to changing circumstances or to move on.

Another aspect is that they come from within. They are determined by one's own needs and anchors, not from conventional assumptions of what shape a career ought to take. In other words, if you do not feel that you want to be a chief executive, or even a main board director, why be driven by someone else's expectations that this is what you should be aiming for?

A simple test is to list the interests you most value in your life, but which you might have to give up or cut down to get to or near the top. Then list the aspects of being at or near the top and attach a score to them. If the first score is appreciably higher than the second score, it does not mean that you do not have the right stuff – but it could mean that you are following someone else's expectations about your career, rather than your own inclinations.

Notes

1 Both internationally acclaimed British architects; Rogers as designer of the Pompidou Centre in Paris and the Lloyd's Building in London; and Stirling as designer of the Fogg Museum at Harvard and the State Gallery in Stuttgart.

2 C. Cox and C. Cooper, High flyers (Basil Blackwell, Oxford, 1988).
3 Korn Ferry and Columbia School of Business, 21st century report: reinventing the CEO (New York and London).
4 P. Kakabadse and P. Dainty, Police chief officers, a management development survey (MCB University Press, Bradford, UK, 1988).
5 A. Jay, Management and Machiavelli (Hodder & Stoughton, London, 1967/ Penguin, London, 1970).
6 Cox and Cooper, High flyers.
7 Andreas Whittam Smith, interviewed in Graduate Post, 13 June 1989.
8 As the Financial Times described him.
9 P. Kakabadse, L. Ludlow and S. Vinnicombe, Working in organisations (Penguin, London, 1988).
10 L. Iacocca, Iacocca, an autobiography (Bantam, New York, 1984).

7

Corporate Horses for
Career Courses

When in December 1988 the fashion retail group Next fired its dynamic chief executive and chairman, George Davies – the man who in less than a decade had turned Hepworth, an out-moded chain of men's retail stores, into a group of boutiques whose innovative style had transformed Britain's high streets – there was endless speculation about what had happened. It was true that the share price had slumped, but so had that of other retail companies whose stores had clearly offered Davies the sincerest form of flattery – imitation – but whose chief executives were still firmly in place. What had Davies done or failed to do, to move so swiftly from champ to apparent chump? What had caused the 'bitter boardroom battles', of the headline writers' cliché?

There was certainly no sense that he was resting on his laurels. 'Every morning at 6 am Davies leapt from his four poster, which is swathed in Next fabrics, to consult the computer showing the daily returns of each of his shops and the *Financial Times* index', an article in *The Times*[1] told us.

The story that soon began to emerge was that he was a typical first-generation entrepreneur who was having trouble handling the next phase of the business he had built up; intuitive, inspirational ('a terrific motivator' in the words of one of his employees), totally involved in everything to do with the business ('What else is there?', he asked *The Times* interviewer in reply to a question about his other interests). Brilliant on ideas, he was impatiently autocratic in their implementation and bored with any talk of obstacles and problems. The name he had chosen for his group, Next, was itself significant. New projects, said one of his associates, were what really interested him most.

These are some of the characteristics that are needed to found a business, but they are not enough to keep it on the rails as it grows and faces competitors. His successor and, according to an article in *The Observer*,[2] the man who had engineered his downfall, was cut from entirely different cloth:

> Jones is a chartered secretary and certified accountant, the legacy of six years of correspondence courses ... (he) is anything but a retailer, more a methodical and orthodox businessman who views the challenges of commerce through the singular eye of an accountant.

Under Davies, being a Next manager had, by all accounts, been like being a member of a family, with a benevolent father figure, whose word was law. It was an arrangement that attracted an impressive degree of commitment, in which people were willing to work 60-hour weeks and sit through all-night meetings. 'Will we do it for our new bosses?', mused one of Next's senior employees after the shake-up: 'They may be financial wizards, but have they got what it takes?'

That is a situation that is liable to be faced by anyone whose career takes them through the exciting early days of the growth of a new enterprise to its next, more organized stage. Similar traumas occurred at Apple when John Sculley – 'the man from Corporate America', as he described himself – arrived to introduce the disciplines that he had learned at Pepsi. Like Next, Apple was a company headed by a visionary leader, Steve Jobs, who treated his employees like a family and whose focus was entirely on new products, in this case the Apple Macintosh; so much so that 'he and his Macintosh cohorts began openly to call everyone else in the company "bozos"'.[3]

It was a recipe for chaos. Steve Jobs, like Davies and many other founder-chief executives (in Britain, Tony Berry of Blue Arrow, Sir Phil Harris of Queensway, and Sir Terence Conran of Storehouse were all cited as examples by *The Economist*[4]) had not adapted himself to the next, more boring, consolidation stage of his company's development. He was trapped in its impetuous youth, where success is based on breaking away creatively from the established way of doing things. The difference between Pepsi and Apple, which is also the difference between two generations of an organization, is summed up by Sculley as follows:

> At Apple the conversation was sprinkled with words like 'vision' and 'values' ... They replaced other words in the vocabulary of the traditional manager, words like 'discipline', 'accountability', 'competition' and 'market wants'.

The natural life of organizations

There is a relationship between career moves and the lifetime development of an organization. In a rough way, the phases that organizations go through also echo the various passages of individual life. Leslie Dighton, a British management consultant who specializes in what he calls 'corporate renewal', has also pointed out that very few corporations last longer in their original form than the biblical three score years and ten of a person's life. The first phase is a transition from youth to stability and maturity. Eventually corporations become set in their ways and go on doing what has worked before, regardless of changes in their environment. Ultimately, if this tendency is not corrected, they weaken and die, although death is often symbolic: it comes in the shape of a takeover, rather than that of the grim receiver. Thus, in its early stages, an organization is a different place to work in from later on, in its mature stage. Career consultants believe that, in making a career move, it is often a good idea to choose a setting that bears the broad correspondence between the stages of individual life, which we talked about in chapter 5, and corporate life.

These latter stages were well described in a paper given by Dr Robert R. Blake, chairman of Scientific Methods Inc. of Austin, Texas, at the Fifth World Congress on Management Development.[5] He saw them as falling into three categories: entrepreneurial, mechanistic and dynamic. The last of these options is not one available to human beings: a revival, usually brought about by a turnaround leader.

The entrepreneurial stage

In fact events at the beginning of the 1990s suggest that there are problems in new, fast-growth companies which have to do with the stock market-driven structure of the economy in all countries except, perhaps, Japan. The roll-call of casualties and stumblers is impressive in its range and geographic spread. To name only a few of the more spectacular examples: Sock Shop (niche retail multiple) and Saatchi & Saatchi (advertising and management consultancy service conglomerate) in Britain; The Bond Corporation (brewery, property and media) in Australia; Campeau (property and prestige retailing) in the USA.

George Davies believes that institutional investors, able to move their money around the world for the best returns at literally the speed of light, expect spectacular performance to grow by arithmetical progression and that this eventually places intolerable pressures on entrepreneurs. 'If you turn in £30 million profit one year, the City expects £50–£60 million the next year', he says. It is at this point that they try to cross 'the bridge too far' by growing too quickly, paying too much for acquisitions, getting too far into expensively funded debt.

The lesson in this is that those who join such companies for a fast career ride and the potential share option rewards that go with it will have to know when to get off. They will also have to have the steely resolve that is needed to break off what often becomes a personal relationship with the highly charismatic bosses that head such companies.

The entrepreneurial stage, as the name implies, represents the founding years of a business. As in the case of Next, says Blake:

> ... the entrepreneurial firm takes its direction and character from the intense drive and determination of the top executive ... The entrepreneur's determination to succeed is boundless. There are not enough hours in the day to satisfy the desired end.

In career terms, he goes on to say, 'working with someone who makes things happen is like an aphrodisiac to those who share the same spirit, and they give their steadfast devotion to this tower of strength'. A *Times* article on Next, quoted by Blake, bears this out in describing the commitment shown by one couple in its junior management:

> We rarely see each other except at weekends which we spend looking round Next shops in other cities. I was a Next Merit Award winner and the prize was a fortnight in Mauritius touring Next factories. We go to sleep dreaming of the Next logo.

Blake points out that the entrepreneurial spirit provides 'an extremely effective way for propelling a new firm on to the corporate scene, or for shifting the character of the old one to regain its competitive edge'. The problem from an employee career, as well as a corporate, point of view is that the character of the entrepreneur often makes him or her ill-equipped to deal with the problems of growth. The inventor–entrepreneur continues to pursue inventions regardless, as Sir Clive Sinclair did, fatally, with his unsuccessful QL computer and then with the disastrous electric car that brought his company to its knees. Even what Blake calls 'the operating entrepreneur' becomes overburdened by the demands of the organization. Commitment is no longer enough. What is needed are order and predictability: that is when the organization has to enter its mechanistic stage and it calls for people like Sculley, 'the man from corporate America' or David Jones, the accountant who succeeded George Davies at Next.

The mechanistic stage

'The heroic style – the lone cowboy on horseback – is not the figure we worship any more at Apple', writes Sculley in describing the painful transformation of the company into its mechanistic stage. Dr Blake puts the process like this:

> The focus of attention must shift from that of a heroic leader commanding the troops to a new regimental order that serves

to guide action. People look back with nostalgia at the excitement and splendour that characterised the free-wheeling period of yesterday.

What takes its place, he says, is 'formal hierarchy, budgeting techniques, job descriptions, organisation charts, procedure manuals, forecasting and an almost endless array of standardised methodologies'. In career terms, there can be a crisis for those who 'find it difficult to buckle under and accept the rigidity of mechanistic procedures'.

These procedures have perils for the organization as well. In his book on what it was like working for IBM,[6] David Mercer describes how the company, in moving from the dynastic phase (Thomas Watson and his son) to a more bureaucratic mode, introduced 'the device of continuous change (to deny the bureaucrats a firm foothold)'. Ultimately it met with only mixed success. IBM, although still an enormously powerful corporation, has been under pressure from new computer companies for the past five years. It was a slow and late entrant to the field of the personal computer, and Mercer thinks that it has never quite adapted itself to the different sales and organizational techniques that this called for. Although not talking specifically about IBM, Blake throws some light on its dilemma – and on the potential career problems of people who work for companies going through a similar phase – in saying that, at this point:

> The strong focus on organisation structure and supplying the business methodologies to make it run smoothly have taken the spotlight off the company's principal products and services and how they fare in the marketplace.

The dynamic stage

The dynamic stage, as we indicated earlier, is usually brought about by the appearance of a turnaround leader, who refocuses objectives (as Allen Sheppard did in taking Grand Metropolitan out of a whole host of what he saw as peripheral activities and concentrating on food and drink), simplifies management structures (as Robert Horton did at BP in stripping out what he called the 'brigadier Belt' of middle management) and changes the way people do their jobs (as Sir John Harvey-Jones did at ICI, by detaching main board directors from narrow functional activities that led to empire building and the pursuit of interests vested in those empires). Harvey-Jones's business autobiography[7] is to a large extent an account of what it takes to transform an organization that had begun to show signs of entering an advanced mechanistic stage back into a dynamic entity.

Being in or entering an organization that is going through a dynamic phase is an exciting career experience for those who can buy into its agenda, and who have the stamina to sustain a fast and furious pace; but it can be an uncomfortable one for those who do not share the vision or the energy. At America's General Electric, the arrival of John F. (Jack) Welch heralded the loss of 100 000 jobs (including 700 out of 1700 headquarters staff) and the introduction of an entirely new breed of manager. 'Much like Welch himself', an article in *Business Week* tells us, 'they thrive on turmoil and turn it to the corporation's advantage'. A senior manager admits that 'what we're doing here isn't for everybody'.[8]

It should be noted, by the way, that dynamic stages can only be orchestrated from the top. A very common unsmart move is going into an organization with the idea that one can change it from lower down. Unless an agenda for change has the whole-hearted commitment of the organization's leaders, it almost always results in the rejection of the change-maker, since the natural state of organizations is to preserve the *status quo* that everyone is comfortable with.

Changing places

Organizations, or even parts of an organization, can also become quite different places to work in at different stages in their development. The same *Business Week* article points out that:

> Once formal, stable, gentlemanly, the new GE is tough, aggressive, iconoclastic. 'It's a brawl,' says Frank P. Doyle, the senior vice-president for corporate relations. 'It's argumentative, confrontational.' Working there can be a shock for newcomers.

In this sense the stages of corporate development are more drastic than those experienced by individuals, who remain basically the same person. That is a vital point to note in career terms. One of the most frequent causes of career problems is when people fail to align the personal development, and the values they have acquired in the course of it, with the developmental stage of the organization they are in or are thinking of joining. Writing about the reasons why the brilliant film director, David Puttnam, took 'one of the biggest Hollywood nosedives on record', *The Economist* wrote that he never understood how the system there worked and that its essentially mechanistic, anti-risk-taking style was quite at odds with the way he himself operated.[9]

Another noted example of the same kind of problem has been the failure of most of the top businessmen who have been brought in by Mrs Thatcher to apply their methods to the cumbersome processes of the Civil Service. 'And so the Whitehall machine has claimed the scalp of yet another businessman', began an article in *Today*,[10] describing the resignation of Victor Paige, the £70 000 a year high-flyer who was recruited to streamline the National Health Service. Unnamed senior civil servants told the reporter that with a few exceptions, none of these government appointees had appreciated 'the need to take policies into account' when trying to get anything done. 'He thought because he was the chief executive he could do as he liked, the same as in an ordinary company', said a Whitehall mandarin of one of these talented outsiders from an alien world: 'Of course he couldn't'.

Career obituaries such as these can, with appropriate variations, be multiplied almost infinitely by career consultants. It is for this reason that Nicholson and West[11] stress the importance of understanding organizations as well as individuals in career planning. Career theorists, they point out, seem to have put all their emphasis on the individual: 'but this will always be unsatisfactorily abstract unless it is grounded in the context of what we know about organisations'.

Organizations and their cultures:
or what are you getting yourself into?

The age of an organization is one of the clues to its 'corporate culture'. That term has been much bandied about in recent years as managers have become aware of the all-embracing importance of 'the way we do things around here': still the least pretentious and best definition. In many industries it 'isn't what they do, but the way that they do it' that gives companies their competitive edge. The chief executive of one very large office equipment manufacturer encapsulated it for us: 'Let's face it, one copier is much like another. The difference is the way we treat our customers'. In other words, the difference lies in the culture of his organization.

Culture also provides the answer to that fundamental career-move question: 'What is X like to work for?' The usual reply is on the lines of 'a typical FMCG outfit', 'a typical bank' or 'a typical Silicon Valley situation'. But it is possible and necessary to be more scientific than that, precisely because the concept of corporate culture has itself become so important in the post-feudal organization. Educationist Anne Jones, well known as a headmistress before becoming a senior civil servant, puts the case in her book, *Leadership for tomorrow's schools*:[12]

> Understanding the connection between the person, the role and the culture is important, both for would-be Heads choosing a school in which they may be able to work productively, and for Head selectors choosing a Head who will be effective rather than disastrous.

For 'Head' one might as well read 'manager', but corporate culture also has a bearing on corporate performance. This was primarily the starting point of Peters and Waterman's bestseller *In search of excellence*. The deceptively simple question they asked themselves was why some organizations performed so much better than others. The answer was not in the products, but in the way they behaved towards people inside and outside the organization.

The efforts of researchers following in Peters and Waterman's footsteps have not always been kindly received by practical business people. The somewhat solemn author of a book called *Managing corporate culture*[13] quotes one exasperated chief executive as telling him: 'This whole culture business is a bunch of bunk. The only culture in this company is in the yoghurt in the cafeteria'. Nevertheless, that negative answer in itself said something about the culture of that company. We would guess that it was being run by a paternalistic autocrat who gave his staff a fair deal, and maybe more, but who was not very interested in their opinions.

Such an organization has what Roger Harrison, in an extremely influential article which first presented the concept of corporate culture to the business community through its publication in 1972 in the *Harvard Business Review*,[14] called a 'power orientation'. Harrison classified organizational cultures as falling into four 'orientations; a word he used to indicate that they seldom ran uniformly all the way through, but that they represented a pre-ponderance of truth about the way each of these different kinds of organizations would be likely to behave.

The categories that he used were 'power', 'role', 'task' and 'person', and they have reappeared in different guises in work by other writers. In a well known book[15] by Professor Charles Handy, who worked with Harrison, they emerge as the 'gods of manage-ment': Zeus, the most important Greek god, represents the power culture; Apollo, the God of Reason, is the patron of the role culture; Athene and Dionysus are the symbols, respectively, of task and person cultures. An easier model to relate to is perhaps the one that appears in Gareth Morgan's, *Images of the organisation*,[16] together with a working explanation of each type:

autocracy (power)	'We'll do it this way'
bureaucracy (role)	'We're supposed to do it this way'
technocracy (task)	'It's best to do it this way'
democracy (person)	'Let's do it together'

(Morgan subdivides the last of these models into 'representative democracy' - we can't do anything until our representatives have voted on it; and 'direct democracy' - we can't do anything until we've voted on it.)

Autocracy (power)

Power cultures are almost always to be seen in the first phase of the life of an organization, when the founder still feels a strong sense of ownership – irrespective of the fact that he or she may only have a minority shareholding. The situation you can expect to find in a power culture is well described by Anne Jones:

> The boss is a leader rather than a manager, a powerful charismatic figure, who works somewhat pragmatically. Such a leader makes decisions more by hunch and a kind of divine intuition than by logic and close reasoning. His staff give whole-hearted and loyal support. His power is unquestioned. Their greatest reward is to please their leader. To the leader is attributed enormous power; the staff are both beguiled by and dependent on their boss as the inspiration for all that they do.

This may sound like a composite portrait of a number of organizations of this kind, but it corresponds remarkably closely to the account we were given by a senior manager in a famous 'power culture' company:

> Everything you've heard about this firm is true. Life is totally unpredictable and you never really know what your job is – or how long you're going to have it. The only thing that is clear is that you're working for the boss and members of his family. They're the only ones who have any real power.
>
> Some of the other managers here play office politics because they think it's going to get them somewhere, but it won't. I can't see the family will ever give real responsibility about anything that matters to anyone outside. The other reason why people play politics is to please the boss, or to get his favourable attention. That can pay off. He's apt to give someone a huge rise because he's seen them do something he approves of. That can have embarrassing consequences – you might find someone who's working for you who's suddenly earning more than you are! On the other hand, it's equally on the cards that you might be at the receiving end of some unpredictable piece of generosity.

The firing rate is pretty high, though equally there are capable managers who've been here for years, even though the boss is notoriously not an easy man to work for. There's no policy, and very little in the way of argument or discussion; not on anything substantive, anyway. It's run entirely on his gut feeling. He's a remarkable man, really. He's brilliant, an incredibly hard worker and he's got enormous charm – though he can also be absolutely foul. He's got an immense ego. That's the secret of his success, but he's also vulnerable in some odd ways; anxious to demonstrate his power to make up for that.

Although it corresponds to what you say is a power culture, it's also quite bureaucratic in some ways. The boss has no time for accountants, but it can take forever to get permission to spend quite small sums of money. That is because everything has to be approved by a member of the family. If they're not around to give a signature, you just can't get an authorisation, not even for an urgent business trip across the Channel.

Apart from those who get fired, the people who leave are the ones who can't take the unpredictability of life here. They come because they think it's going to be different, or perhaps they're told it's going to be different, but it never is. Funnily enough women seem to be able to handle the situation here better than men. Perhaps because they're used to life being unfair![17]

When I was approached by the company, I at first told them I wasn't interested. I was doing pretty well where I was. Eventually I really went along to meet the boss because I'd heard so much about him, and I was intrigued. But like everyone who meets him on that basis, I was totally won over.

Of course, we've had terrible rows since then, but I enjoy it. I like drama, and working here is often like taking part in a soap opera. I'd rather have that than the grey, predictable lives some of my contemporaries have. Also my job happens to be very interesting and the money is pretty good.

The big question in my mind is what happens when the boss dies. He's a larger than life figure who seems to defy mortality, but even he can't do that – at least I don't think so!

I think he's going to find it hard to give up power, even to members of the family who are being groomed for it. I suppose the whole thing might just eventually disintegrate. In career terms that's the risk you take in a power culture.

One of the points that this executive made was that some of the managers who had been with the company a long time felt a tremendous debt of gratitude to the founder of the business. Financially, and as a learning experience in working for a man who was undoubtedly a brilliant business leader, this feeling was certainly well founded. On the other hand, in career terms, there is a problem embedded in such a relationship because it can ultimately create a sense of dependency in a subordinate. We will examine this theme further in chapter 10.

Bureaucracy ('role')

In turning to an accountant as its chief executive, Next may be entering the classic second phase of organizations. When this happens, says Roger Harrison, there is 'in contrast to the wilful autocracy of the power-oriented organisation . . . a preoccupation with legality, legitimacy and responsibility'. The emphasis is now on the system, and each worker has a clearly defined role in relation to the job itself and to his or her position in the hierarchy. Rights, privileges and status marks accumulate. Things tend to get done 'by the book' and, in fact, role cultures encourage people to work that way because they thrive on standardization. The dominant ethic is how you do it, not how effectively you do it; or, as Harrison puts it, there is a tendency 'to place procedural correctness before task effectiveness'. That may not be explicitly stated, but it is the underlying theme.

The Civil Service, banks, insurance companies and large stable organizations are all examples of role cultures. A senior official gave us a good snapshot picture of life in a typical bank:

> Ranks at [XYZ] Bank follow loosely the model of the military and the Civil Service. People that get to the top are those that please the system – not the customer; or at least, the only customers they're interested in are large accounts. That's at odds with the expensive advertising campaign we're running

which stresses the very opposite message. The only consolation is that the other banks are no better.

Status symbols abound at [XYZ]. These days it's the size and make of the company car, though until recently status was signalled by room size, type of desk and the quality of the desk set. We're more democratic now, but there's a definite delineation of sub-hierarchies in the make of radio in the car.

The reason why our mutual friend Mr Y won't get anywhere, even though he's bright and speaks fluent French and Spanish, is that he's too much of an oddball. He's not the management's idea of the manager of a major branch, and that's an essential step on the way up.

Technocracy ('task')

Whereas in role cultures, process ('how') is the important issue, in task cultures, it is the product – getting it done is what matters. In another influential article on the theme of corporate culture in the *Harvard Business Review*,[18] Professor Henry Mintzberg says that such an organization:

> . . . relies for its operating tasks on trained professionals – skilled people who must be given considerable control over their own work . . . As a result the structure emerges as very decentralised; power over many decisions, both operating and strategic, flows all the way down the hierarchy to the professionals of the operating core. For them this is the most democratic structure of all.

It is in task organizations that one finds a trend towards putting together 'task forces' to solve problems, and where leadership comes from project managers, rather than from hierarchies. Task forces are often disbanded when a new project comes up, and there is comparatively little sense of cohesion among the members of the organization as a whole, except in relation to the specific purpose of the job in hand. Mintzberg mentions, as a case in point, a five-hour operation observed by one of his colleagues in which the surgeon and the anaesthetist did not exchange a single word.

Management consultancies are classic examples of 'task' organizations. In career terms this type of setting suits those who are extremely confident of their professional skills, but who take a rather dispassionate and uninvolved view of the people they work with. Comradeship is not something you find much of in task organizations. A young management consultant described his working environment and its career implications as follows:

> The accent is very much on self management and an aspect of that is to get into a 'hot' area of consultancy. There's a lot of competition to get into the right teams, which means catching the attention of the project managers who make up the teams. It's a bit like picking sides for an informal game of football at school. If you consistently get picked last, you're not long for this world here. It's an 'up or out' culture. The other thing is that you're very much judged on how much chargeable time you can clock up. Training and career development doesn't count to that end, so you have to do it in your own time. There's not much socialising after work. We're much too busy for that.

In career terms, what he says is substantiated by Roger Harrison's findings: 'Status and recognition', he says in his *Harvard Business Review* article, 'depend almost entirely on task contribution'. He also adds the warning note that even when this is of a high order it is not a guarantee of continuing employment: 'When his knowledge and skills become obsolete ... an individual is expected to step gracefully aside to make room for someone who is better qualified'.

Democracy ('person')

Person cultures are often found in professional partnerships, where everyone has complementary qualifications of more or less equal value. 'The organisation exists primarily to serve the needs of its members', says Harrison, who describes it as 'a device through which the members can meet needs they could not otherwise satisfy by themselves ... Consensus methods of decision making are preferred; people are generally not expected to do things that are incongruent with their own goals and values'.

This sounds very agreeable, but in reality person cultures have a nasty habit of breaking apart. The journal of the Royal Institute of British Architects, for instance, is full of small news items about dissolving partnerships as well as of those being formed. Those that last are often dominated by one strong personality.

Person cultures can be a pitfall for outsiders, those who do not belong to the charmed circle of those with the 'right' professional qualifications. In recent years, for instance, some professional firms have realized the need to be more business-like and have taken on highly paid general managers with administrative qualifications, such as in law or accountancy, or with general business experience. These appointments often do not work because of a clash between the person culture of the organization concerned and the bureaucratic processes that such managers feel they need to put into place in order to do the job they were appointed to do.

Person cultures are also frequently found in the early years of business enterprises which are formed by a number of individuals sharing a high degree of specialized knowledge. This situation was very much in evidence when John Sculley arrived at Apple. The decision-making process, he says, was one in which almost everyone felt entitled to participate by virtue of the quality of their computer expertise. He found that, ultimately, he could not run what had become a large company on this ultra-democratic model. The pitfalls emerged at an early meeting to discuss corporate strategy:

> The meeting became a free for all. Whoever could distract the group's attention controlled the floor. It was difficult to distinguish between facts and opinions. People would have side conversations during executive presentations ... It became clear this wasn't a team at all: that we had a group of individuals all running their own functions.

Sculley's appointment eventually led to the downfall of Steve Jobs, who had started the company and who had appointed him. But it was a close-run thing, even for a man who was clearly a very tough operator. His wife posed a question right at the beginning that every ambitious outsider entering a culture with a founder (power) or a set of founders (person) should ask themselves. 'He started this company', she said, speaking of Jobs: 'What makes you think in a million years that you're going to have a free hand to run it?'

Sculley's book is full of morals about the importance of self-knowledge, both for those who join person cultures and for those who invite what sometimes turn out to be Trojan horses from corporate life to join them. Their values may well turn out to be at odds with those expressed by one of the close associates of Alan Ladd Jr, the American film producer, in a fascinating interview published in the *Harvard Business Review*.[19] He sums up one of the essential characteristics of the person culture in saying 'I get up in the morning and I look forward to seeing the people and exchanging ideas. It's as much the actual way we all work together that is important to me, beyond the product'.

Organization shapes and career patterns

Although we stress once again that the various types of organization described by writers such as Handy, Harrison, Mintzberg and others are 'orientations', not absolutes, they do seem to correspond with the perception that people have of the places they work in.

Another important perception is that they correspond roughly with the phases of the life of organizations. Power (autocracy) and person (democracy) cultures are found in the early stages. Role culture (bureaucracy) is the next phase, as at IBM where, as David Mercer tell us,[20] 'after more than half a century of idiosyncratic and paternalistic rule, the dynasty [i.e. Tom Watson Sr and Jr] handed over to the bureaucrats'. Task culture (technocracy) is often the one found in a revitalizing phase, when the organization is going through a process of renewing its energies and re-tooling its response to the outside world. Then, says Anne Jones,[21] 'The driving force is not power and glory, nor efficiency and control, but rather getting the job done, with particular emphasis on redefining the task according to the needs of the situation'.

The scope that task organizations give to individuals to exercise their skills and deploy what are sometimes under-used talents, and the flexibility of project teams – the way in which they can be assembled and disbanded in relation to market needs – makes them an ideal configuration for dealing with change and in-stability. These are the conditions that organizations are facing in the 1990s, and highly respected commentators such as Charles Handy and Tom Peters see the task model as the pattern of the future. So should one seek such organizations out in planning one's career?

Our answer could be summed up in a guarded 'well, yes'. For one thing it depends on the *doing* skills and *being* attributes to which we referred in chapter 3. A task culture, as we have shown, can be a bleak place for those whose doing skills are not quite up to those of the best of their peers, or whose being attributes attach a high value to order, systems and predictability. They might actually be better off in a role culture in which steady competence is regarded more highly than a flow of brilliant but sometimes awkward ideas. Similarly, a person culture might be a better place for someone who passionately feels that the way they interact with their colleagues is more important than the product, as is the case at the Ladd Company.

A further point to bear in mind is that task organizations do not seem to stay that way. The natural development of organizations, towards what biologists call their 'climax vegetation', almost in-variably leads to a role culture. Eventually, says Mintzberg:[22]

The innovative consulting firm converges on a few of its most successful products, packing them into standard skills, and settles down to life as a professional bureaucracy; the manu-facturer of prototypes hits on a hot product and becomes a machine bureaucracy to produce it.

Very successful people – and that includes those who have defined success in their own terms, not necessarily those who have got to the top on a conventional view – make the point that they have had an instinct for when to stay and when to go. Con-versely, less successful ones, Nicholson and West found, tended to be overtaken by events. The instinct for moving at the right time has a close bearing on being able to sense changes in the shape and destiny of the organization: for example, when a power culture, where argument and discussion is not welcomed, starts to get out of touch with its environment; or when a task culture starts to develop a middle-age spread of hierarchies and status symbols.

But even these orientations do not run right through the organization. You cannot rely on finding consistent behaviour throughout the organization. In the power culture we described earlier, there was also a typical role, or bureaucratic, set of procedures for obtaining permission to spend quite small amounts of money. Equally, it is possible to find a power culture operating within a person one. Peter Willingham, a headhunter who recruits managers for professional practices, says that although these are ostensibly archetypal person cultures, the real power very often lies with one dominant personality or group – who may or may not be the titular head. The success of a newcomer to such a scene will depend almost entirely on whether he or she has sized up the situation correctly.

The age of the organization, the industry it is in and what you know of its reputation do tell you a lot about the culture you are likely to find. But the fit is not absolute and there are no easy-to-read labels to guide you; rather, the lettering on the labels only becomes clear to the untrained eye once you are a member of the organization. Sadly, even if the evidence is there already, people do not always draw the right conclusion from it. To give a very simple example: if you are a person who works from a cluttered desk, and your introduction to the organization you are thinking of joining takes you past offices where people mostly have a screen and one piece of paper in front of them, you may have a problem fitting into their culture. Therefore one of the career skills that you need is to be a cultural detective. There are ways in which the look of the place and the people in it provide strong clues to which of the four cultural orientations we have described is likely to be the predominant one. That is the subject of our next chapter.

Executive summary

Smart career moves are not only a matter of fitting the 'doing' qualities of the job in question. The importance that is increasingly being attached to the notion of corporate culture makes it necessary to put at least equal weight on making the right connection between personal development, personal values and the culture of the organization. This is a crucial factor in whether you can actually get anything done in a career move to a new setting.

The age of the organization generally determines how it is likely to behave: impetuous, fast-moving and entrepreneurial in its early years; and more mechanical, bureaucratic and system-oriented as it grows. In its third stage it will either renew its youthful energies in a turnaround episode, or it will gradually break up when it becomes too slow and cumbersome to react to its environment.

There is a connection between these various characteristics and the corporate culture that one is likely to encounter. Cultures fall into four main types: power (autocracy), role (bureaucracy), task (technocracy) and person (democracy).

Some of these types are related to the lifespan of the organization: power, task and, in some cases (e.g. professional practices), person cultures predominate in the early years, while role characteristics take over in the next phase. The renewal stage is often marked by a return to a power culture. The alternative is anarchy, which might be termed an extreme and highly unstable form of democracy.

There is also a connection between organizational development and personal lifespan characteristics. Most younger people prefer task and person cultures, where results count rather than following procedures. The greater stability of bureaucratic, role cultures is often a more suitable setting in the later stages of a career. Autocracy is more of a puzzle: how one fares in such a setting depends, more than in any other culture, on personal chemistry with one individual – the autocrat him- or herself. But in career as well as in personal terms, it is necessary to break away from the father figure of the autocrat at some point in order to develop.

The term 'culture' suggests stability, or at least some kind of long-term fixture, but this is not necessarily the case with corporate cultures. They can change very suddenly, for instance, with a change of management, as happened at Apple when Steve Jobs's person culture was replaced by Sculley's mix of task and power cultures. It is important to look out for signs of culture change in organizations – or signs of changes in one's own values. Either may signify that one's face no longer fits.

Notes

1 'Where two is company', *The Times*, 19 December 1988.
2 'The man who ousted George Davies', *The Observer*, 18 December 1988.
3 J. Sculley, *Odyssey: Pepsi to Apple* (Harper & Row, New York, 1987).
4 'Britain's hares and tortoises', *The Economist*, 25 March 1989.
5 *World Congress on Management Development* (MCB University Press, Bradford, UK, 1988).
6 D. Mercer, *IBM: how the world's most successful organisation is managed* (Kogan Page, London, 1987).
7 Sir John Harvey-Jones, *Making it happen* (Collins, London, 1988).
8 'Jack Welch: how good a manager?', *Business Week*, 14 December 1987.
9 'Take two', *The Economist*, 3 December 1988.
10 'Throttled by red tape', *Today*, 5 June 1986.
11 N. Nicholson and M. West, *Managerial job change: men and women in transition* (Cambridge University Press, 1988).
12 A. Jones, *Leadership for tomorrow's schools* (Basil Blackwell, Oxford, 1987).
13 S. M. Davis, *Managing corporate culture* (Harper & Row, New York, 1984).
14 'Understanding your organisation's character', *Harvard Business Review*, May–June 1972.
15 C. Handy, *The gods of management* (Pan Books, London, 1978).
16 G. Morgan, *Images of the organisation* (Sage, Beverly Hills, California and London, 1986).
17 There is an interesting comment on this in Michael Korda's *Male chauvinism: how it works at home and in the office* (Simon & Schuster, New York/Coronet, London, 1972). In a family-dominated organization, he says, it is more effective for women to behave like members of the family: 'drama, tears, rage and an appeal to personal justice are likely to be more effective, whereas forming a committee would seem like a hostile and treacherous act'.

18 H. Mintzberg, 'Organisation design: fashion or fit?', *Harvard Business Review*, January–February 1981.

19 'When friends run the business', *Harvard Business Review*, July–August 1980.

20 Mercer, IBM.

21 Jones, *Leadership for tomorrow's schools*.

22 Mintzberg, 'Organisation design: fashion or fit?'.

8

Corporate Culture: the Hidden Messages That Say it All

The culture of organizations, as we have seen in the last chapter, determines how they behave towards employees and customers, how they react to events and how pro-active they are. These are all important factors in evaluating the potential of a career move.

For the outsider, information about culture comes partly through anecdote, partly by way of experience and partly through visual impressions. The problem with the first two ways of finding out about the culture is that anecdotes are apt to be imprecise and that experience can only be gained once you are a member of the organization. Visual impressions, on the other hand, can be a very immediate and powerful way of communicating what the culture is.

But there is a big proviso. In his influential book, *The presentation of self in everyday life*,[1] the American sociologist Erving Goffman describes the various ways in which individuals, consciously or otherwise, stage-manage the impression they make on others, in order to project the image they have of themselves, or at any rate how they would like others to see them. He points out that this is often at odds with reality: 'The "true" or "real" attitudes, beliefs or emotions of the individual can be ascertained only indirectly . . . through what appears to be involuntary expressive behaviour.'

That behaviour generally takes the form of 'body language', more technically known as 'non-verbal communication' – a process whereby people unintentionally give the game away about how they really feel about themselves and others, by involuntary gesture, tone of voice or physical attitude. These 'involuntary gestures' are more significant than the impression an observer is 'supposed' to get.

The body language of organizations

Organizations and their managers also have intended and unintended ways of communicating their values and attitudes, both to outsiders and to employees. At a very simple level, even the choice of location is significant. The headquarters of Wal-Mart, America's most profitable and fastest growing retail group, is a nondescript building in Arkansas, one of the less glamorous US states. Low cost, not high style, is what counts in an organization like that. In Europe, moving the headquarters of a major public company from an expensive downtown office to an unfashionable suburb, or to a green-field site, is a common way of signalling a change in priorities and management style.

But it is the look of the buildings themselves that is most significant. Banks, for instance, communicate solidity: most people would feel worried by one that looked like a design studio, whereas the clients of a design studio would probably be unhappy if it were to look as solid and stolid as a bank. The head offices of many large corporations, says designer Wally Olins, cultivate anonymity to create the impression of a 'quiet powerhouse, run by some benign superintelligence which can predict and control the business environment'.[2] He also points out that large, complex organizations try to give a visual impression of order and simplicity, whereas smaller ones often try to suggest that they house a lively variety of different activities and options. John A. Seiler summed it all up in a *Harvard Business Review* article:[3] 'A building gives occupants and visitors messages about what the company does, how it works and what it believes in'. But he added, 'Buildings communicate these messages regardless of the management's intentions'.

Although organizations are increasingly aware of design and what it can do for them, in the majority of cases, certainly in the

UK, the messages given by buildings are not the result of a conscious process at all. The buildings, the layout of the spaces within them and the way they are furnished do, however, express – often in an extremely revealing way – the attitudes you can expect to find once you join that organization. Sheena Wilson, a British sociologist who conducted a survey of building use by 22 leading companies,[4] writes that she was impressed by 'the transparent way in which the building imparted a strong sense of how the company carries out its business and the values it stood for'. Such information is invaluable for those thinking of joining a particular organization.

In a discussion with us she gave, as an example, the different arrangements at two companies she visited:

At company X [the subsidiary of a large PLC] I was kept waiting by a security guard in a gatehouse filled with stale cigarette smoke. Old tabloid newspapers were scattered round a cheap wooden table and the chairs looked as though they had been thrown out by the works canteen.

When I eventually got in to see the management, the meeting took place in a room with a haphazardly set out display of their products in a dusty glass cupboard. The ashtrays round the table looked as though they had been nicked from a pub. This particular firm relies on very large contracts from a few customers over whom they take a lot of trouble. But they don't bother with the rest, which on this evidence would make them rather vulnerable if they lost one of their big contracts.

At company Y, I was treated as a guest. When I arrived, they had an agenda ready for me. The reception area was comfortably furnished and well laid out, I was brought good coffee – in a cup, not a plastic beaker – the company literature on the table was attractively produced and up to date. Company Y is highly successful and is one of the companies cited as an example in Peters and Waterman's *In search of excellence*.

Company Y was probably making an effort to create an effect of caring for its customers. A wishful view of company X's attitude, by someone thinking of joining it, might be that it was so task-oriented that it did not bother with niceties. But it is more likely that indifference and lack of systematic thinking is really its style.

Another very interesting and revealing phenomenon that can be observed is when there is a discrepancy between the way the organization presents itself and its unintentional body language. That suggests that the management does not entirely believe what it says: that it is trying to impress someone by putting over a certain view of itself that is different from reality (in individual terms one might call that hypocrisy).

A notable example is that of a hard-nosed US construction and design company which has established an office in London. It is in a pretty Georgian square and in an elegant building of the same period. But once you go inside, you find that the generous-sized rooms have been partitioned off into pokey spaces and that, in some of them, the beautiful moulded plaster ceilings have been boarded over to house the wiring for overhead strip lighting. Very sensible, of course, but why did they bother with such a building in the first place? 'We thought it would make us more acceptable to the Brits', explained its US chief executive.

A similar motive is probably behind the way some tough financial service companies are located in Georgian buildings around Edinburgh's Charlotte Square, once the intensely con-servative residential heart of that city. The real culture of such organizations is to be found in the way they use the spaces, not in the way the facades look.

Such discrepancies may also point to the fact that the vision at the top is divided, or is not shared by all the members of the organization. Many observers think that the controversial high-tech building in the City that houses Lloyd's of London is a spectacular example of this. It is a gleaming arrangement of pipes and ducts which looks like a gigantic model of the engine of a high-performance car in a glass case. But inside, the 'waiters' (mainly internal messengers), who are the traditional servants of Lloyd's, are still dressed in the uniform of the nineteenth century – frock coats with scarlet facings.

On the main floor, the underwriters continue to work in paper-strewn 'boxes', consisting of two facing rows of benches with a table in the middle. This layout harks back to the seating in eighteenth-century coffee houses, which is how Lloyd's began. But the space which houses the 'boxes' is a huge glass and steel atrium, many stories high, which would not look out of place at NASA.

Almost everywhere one looks, there are indications of a cultural clash between technology and tradition. That impression was confirmed by a report in *The Independent* at the time when the building was opened by the Queen: 'Within Lloyd's', it said, 'there is a mixture of progress and reaction in the way the market conducts its affairs'.[5] The winning side in this struggle, which it would be important to identify if one was thinking of working there, may be indicated by the members' suite at the top of the building. This was not designed by Richard Rogers, the architect of Lloyd's, but by an interior designer who was commissioned separately by its underwriting establishment. It has been fitted out with the kind of bland commercial conservatism that you might see in the lobby of a very expensive hotel.

Another instance of the way in which the appearance of a building can suggest the advent of problems in the organization that it houses was given by Bernard Levin in a light-hearted but perceptive *Times* article:[6]

Shortly after TV-am [Britain's first breakfast television station] was launched, I visited its premises; as I walked into the front hall, alive with fountains, shrubs and flowers, I knew that disaster impended and soon afterwards it struck. How did I know? Well, how do I know that a theatre with huge and lavish dressing rooms will shortly be a multi-storey car park? Because no good work will be done in the world of the arts, the universities or politics if the practitioners are comfortable.

Chemical analysis

Visitors to organizations are generally vaguely aware of the impressions that the feel of a place makes on them, and they draw inferences from that about the way the people who work there are likely to behave. These inferences come under the loose heading of 'vibes'; something about the place that makes you feel either at home or uneasy, depending on your personal style. Headhunters talk of it as 'the chemistry' and for them it is a crucial part of determining whether the candidate they are putting forward is likely to have the right 'being' characteristics to succeed in that environment.

Because managers attach less importance to the 'being' characteristics of a job than to its 'doing' ones, they often ignore these gut feelings. But the vast majority of career problems arise not because people cannot do the job, but because of a chemical mismatch on the being aspects, either between the organizational culture and their personal style or between individuals.

A typical instance was that of Julia Keene (not her real name). After a successful three-year stint with a blue chip multinational consumer goods group, she used a legacy to finance a year-long career break to do an MBA. She was then immediately offered a job by a small, highly regarded management consultancy at nearly twice the money she had earned before.

'We haven't got anyone here with the kind of corporate line management experience you've had', the managing director told her: 'Most of us have come from some form of consultancy'. She was struck by the fact that his office, which seemed almost identical to that of the other consultants, was quite small and more like a large cubicle. In fact, the interviews she had attended took place in a meeting room, and a lot of the working spaces seemed to be open access, rather like those in a reference library.

At the interview she asked who she would be reporting to. 'We don't actually operate like that', the managing director told her: 'It's more like a networking process. We form teams of people to work together on assignments. Sometimes we have different teams working on different assignments that are going on at the same time for different clients. That's why we have almost as many meeting rooms as individual offices'.

Although she could handle the consultancy role intellectually, it was a way of working she could never get used to. She found it impossibly untidy and she was bothered by the fact that she was never given any clear task by anyone. 'Could you look over this and see what you think?', was a frequent approach as someone handed her a thick wadge of documents.

Her colleagues seemed irritated by her desire to be more methodical and specific. She found it annoying when they were 'hogging' the firm's

computer – this was in 1985, when not everyone had a PC. The suggestion then was that she might tackle something else in the meantime, but
she preferred to work through a task methodically, from start to finish.
The managing director told her he was disappointed by the fact that she
was not bringing any new work into the firm: 'We'd really like you to get
about more. Why don't you invite some of your contacts out to lunch
and see if there's anything we ought to be pitching for?'

None of this was really her style, she felt. After 18 rather unhappy
months she went back into the more conventional work settings she
was used to, which involved hierarchies, roles and clearly defined tasks
that could be tackled without interruption.

Julia's competence was not in question: it was simply that the
setting was wrong for her, although for a lot of people it might
have been just right. Could any of her problems have been foreseen? The physical setting of the consultancy which she had noted
at the interview should have given her a clue about its workstyle,
which was very typical of a task or person culture. It was very
similar to that observed by John Sculley when he went to Apple.
He was struck by the extreme informality of the place and the lack
of any corporate status symbols – though oddly enough there
were plenty of private ones in the shape of high-performance cars
in the car park. In other words, there were a lot of people at Apple
with the kind of personal expertise that enabled them to earn a lot
of money at an early age. That too would be an indication of the
kind of organizational setting such people would seek – a college
of peers rather than a hierarchy. It was a situation that caused him
many problems when he tried to run Apple under Steve Jobs.

Role culture people whose career anchors tug them towards
stability and who prefer predictability in the way they work are
often misfits in person or power cultures. These two have their
own, usually unmistakable, footprint. 'You can tell what this place
is like to work in from the look of it', an editor in a publishing
house told us. It was indeed wonderfully untidy and reflected its
driving entrepreneur–owner's impatience and frequent changes of
mind and mood:

You have to be ready to be switched from one job to the next
before you've finished anything – that's why there's so many

documents and files piled around the place. Jim Roth [an accountant who was brought in to impose some much needed systems] couldn't cope with this at all. He liked everything neat and tidy. He really couldn't handle Bill [the owner]. I doubt whether he could change, even if he wanted to. He owns the business, so what he says goes – and his style is interventionist, to say the least.

What you see is what you get

Without setting absolute rules, it is possible to draw up a notation of the way space is used which corresponds roughly to the four different culture types to which usage would relate, and which you might therefore expect to meet; power (we'll do it this way), role (we're supposed to do it this way), task (it's best to do it this way) and person (let's do it together).

Location

Power organizations are controlled by one strong individual, or at least a close-knit group of people, at the top. Another characteristic of such organizations is that they are either in the first phase of their life or are going through a process of corporate renewal under a strong new leader.

In the latter case, we have seen that quite often a physical move is a way of signalling that the culture ('the way we do things around here') is going to change. That usually means a move away from a large, centrally located headquarters building to a smaller, decentralized one – the kind of place where one will find first-phase power organizations. Typical locations for these are industrial estates, converted buildings in run-down suburbs or lower-rent office buildings on the fringe of more expensive areas. In London, for instance, such companies can be found occupying nondescript 1960s office buildings on the other side of the Thames from the City. The main criteria for their choice is a mix of low rentals and strictly functional convenience. They are often close to, but not on, public transport routes and a long way from such amenities as shops and restaurants.

Role organizations are almost the reverse of this. Although costs are forcing them out of downtown areas, you almost always find that the real power base – their core functions – are in a prestige central location. For this reason, role culture headquarters buildings tend to be larger than they need be and to house more executives than is strictly necessary: consider places such as London's Shell Building, the headquarters of the major banks and insurance companies and government offices. If the corridors of power are clearly in one main location, then the members of the organization will try to stay close to them and will resist all efforts to move them away.

Task and *person* organizations are often located in areas in which amenity values have clearly been kept in mind, because the kind of workers they need to attract are highly educated, often younger people with a developed awareness of the quality of life: hence the popularity among such firms of Silicon Valley and the New England states in the USA; and the Thames Valley and the area around Cambridge in the UK. The other factor in this choice of location is that task and person cultures are in many cases associated with knowledge-based sunrise industries – hence they need to be near universities and research establishments.

Buildings

Power cultures pay little attention to design quality, unless the owners are themselves interested in it or it has some connection with the business they are in. According to Tom Peters, the headquarters of Wal-Mart Stores is in the same undistinguished commercial building that it was in a decade ago, during which time the company has grown into the largest retail group in the USA.

Peters adds that what he calls 'the terrible Taj Mahal phenomenon' has not set in at Wal-Mart. By this he presumably means the kind of thing embodied in Sculley's description of the Pepsi headquarters – a *role* culture building on a heroic scale: 'A long meandering driveway through manicured lawns, sculpture gardens and fountains brings you to the Pepsi complex of buildings . . . you feel as though you're at the most important company in the world.'

Not all role culture buildings are as grand as this, of course. Some are merely depressing, such as the glass and concrete cliffs which house some Civil Service departments in London, or the monstrous Home Office building, designed by the then fashionable architect Sir Basil Spence, which looms over St James's Park. In fact, another sign of a role culture is that its buildings express the conventional corporate architectural taste of the period in which they were built. In the 1980s one could see the same trend in the rash of 'post-modern' designs for new corporate headquarters buildings.

Task buildings, on the other hand, are more adventurous, and are more likely to show signs of having been designed by an architect who consulted the users, not just the building owners. They are therefore more likely to have been purpose-built, rather than being one of those speculative slabs, popular in the 1960s and 1970s, which were put up by a developer who then went looking for tenants.

Such buildings are to be found all over the world. One of the best known expressions of their opposite, buildings designed in consultation with a task-oriented workforce, is the Zentralbeheer office in the Netherlands. It is designed as a cluster of small cell-like, highly personalized workspaces, broken up by numerous meeting areas. A similar effect can be seen at the British leisure conglomerate Virgin, whose various divisions camp in a group of small, more or less neighbouring buildings. The idea is to create and maintain a sense of identity within each of its companies. Julia Keene found that this is an accurate reflection of the way task cultures operate, although purpose-designed offices on these lines are as yet rare. It is more common to see the presence of task or role culture reflected in the way the spaces are used (see the next section).

Person cultures, as we pointed out previously, are a feature of the early years of an organization's life. Therefore they are often to be found in buildings that seem, from the outside, to be rather unconventional; for instance, conversions of factory buildings to a different commercial use. Fitness for purpose is one criterion and cost is another, but wit and imagination is usually an essential ingredient.

Another aspect of the person culture is that it is 'owned' by all or most of the people who work for it; professional practices are typical examples. Therefore person culture buildings are sometimes wilfully idiosyncratic. They reflect their users' view of how business ought to be conducted, rather than practicality. That is why, in London, cramped, Dickensian chambers near the Law Courts are a preferred location for legal firms, and why top medical consultants occupy rooms in Harley Street, where the multiplicity of names on the bell pulls suggest that conditions must be as crowded as in a multi-occupancy rooming house.

Internal layouts

The phrase 'corridors of power' is a term that attaches to corridors that literally exist, and they are usually to be found on the upper floors of the building. That location symbolizes the superior status and separateness of those who have, also literally, made it to the top. Their position is often reinforced by the presence of a 'guardian', a secretary or PA, through whose office one has to pass before meeting the person being guarded. The signal such layouts give, says the American management consultant Fritz Steele, is the rejectionist 'we'll call you when we need you'.

In such cultures, managers lower down the hierarchy will often mimic the territorial behaviour of the power leader or top role group. Fritz Steele has noticed that 'individual executives frequently recreate the executive row layout in their own area'.[7] In other cases, they will delineate and mark off status by whatever means comes to hand; for instance, by surrounding themselves with physical barriers such as filing cabinets to cordon off their personal space in an open-plan office.

In fact, the deployment of space plays a very important part in role and power cultures. A number of commentators have noted how the favoured positions in offices are on the periphery near the windows and that corner offices with windows on two sides are the most favoured of all.

Empire building is also a matter of physically extending personal space. In his book on *Power*,[8] Michael Korda advises that careers ought to expand laterally rather than vertically, and that really clever power players do this by physically claiming more and more working space for their activities. Certainly one notices how, in some offices that must have been open plan at one time, departments mark their territory by signs, notices and posters that seem as definite a statement as customs posts at international boundaries.

This can often be a sign that an organization, or some part of it, is making a transition towards becoming a role or power culture. When this happens, the open spaces in which casual and informal meetings take place are likely to be colonized by power seekers; rather in the same way that landlords in the eighteenth century asserted their dominance by enclosing communal spaces in villages.

Conversely, one of the signs which clearly indicates the presence of a *task* or *person* culture, in which people operate as equal members of a peer group, is the existence of numerous areas for open encounters and informal exchanges of views. The new breed of skilled para-professionals, Steele writes, work in a way in which they can circulate, stimulate each other and gather informally to solve problems. The result is apt to disturb those who prefer tidiness in their environment. Dr Frank Duffy, a leading architect who has taken a particular interest in what Steele calls 'organisational ecology', sums up the scene in a *Management Today* article[9] which is also indicative of the attitude of a typical person culture manager to those with role culture attitudes:

> Neatness and order are appropriate for low-paid nine to fivers. Stimulus, excitement and commitment may be much more appropriate messages to convey visually to enthusiastic multi-disciplinary teams in a high tech firm in Silicon Valley [or Silicon Glen].

Another sign is that spaces, whether these are separate offices or areas in an open-plan workplace, are not hierarchically ordered: that is to say that there is often no immediately obvious difference between the space occupied by a senior executive and someone of a more junior rank, because such organizations are flat pyramids of complementary peer groups, rather than hierarchies and ladders.

Workspace furniture, decor and lighting

The provision of furniture and decor comes low in the priorities of the early, power-culture phase of an organization, and it shows. A typical case is that of the fast-growing British construction conglomerate visited in the course of research for this book. It has been assembled into a multi-million pound publicly quoted company by a driven entrepreneurial chief executive in the past ten years or so, through mergers, acquisitions and a breathtaking pace of internal expansion. That is indicated by a constant process of rebuilding and partitioning of individual offices in its head-quarters – but not, frankly, to a high standard. The workmanship has a lowest-tender look about it and the workspaces themselves are overcrowded.

Another sign of that organization's priorities is that although the electronic hardware is to a high standard, the furniture, even that in the chairman's office, looks as though it has been bought piecemeal from the office suppliers down the road – except for some heavy Edwardian pieces that must have come from one of the company's acquisitions. Everything about the company indicates that what is going to count there, in career terms, is performance and cost control, not style. The question is whether the rewards will eventually be fairly distributed when the pay-off comes.

The fact that the chairman's office is as spartan as that of his subordinates is a promising indication and probably makes such an environment acceptable to them. On the other hand, power culture organizations which boast expensive antiques and furniture in their top executive offices, while the staff below slum and swelter, are signs to beware of for those contemplating join-ing them – unless you are quite clearly going to be in the top team. According to Michael Korda, 'extremes in office decoration are usually a sign that it is difficult for a newcomer to obtain power'.

It is also possible to read quite a lot into the values and manage-ment style of the office occupant from the decor that he or she has chosen. Occupational psychologist Adrian Furnham pointed out in an article in *The Guardian*[10] that power is now increasingly signalled by downsizing. Information has always been the basis of power. But as the 'containers' of information have become more compact, the need for large offices and imposing desks has become less functional and more an expression of the occupant's ego – or insecurity. One of the most imposing chief executive offices that we visited underlined this point. The company was quite a small one but his desk was massive, and the walls were covered with photographs of him meeting the great and the good. Another chief executive (chairman of a large property company) demonstrated a different set of values altogether. Pride of place in his office was given to a charming architectural drawing, which he had picked up for 14 shillings (70p) in a junk shop in the 1960s. Which of those two people one would prefer to work for is a matter of personal choice – but both are powerful expressions of non-verbal communication.

In power cultures, few spaces other than those of the power holders and their mimics show much sign of having had thought devoted to them. The reverse is true of *role* cultures. Chairs, desks and other equipment, for instance, are often of a uniform make, purchased through some central agency as part of a corporate procurement policy. But a sure sign of a role culture is when the quality of the furniture, and the size and decor of the offices in which people sit, are related to their status in the hierarchy.

In *person* and *task* cultures one is likely to see the very opposite effect. 'Everyone here worked in small, cramped cubicles, almost as if they were part of a medieval guild', Sculley wrote of his first impression of Apple Computers. That effect is characteristic of many similar organizations. Workspaces are generally more crowded than in role cultures, whose bureaucratic ways ensure that norms of space usage are observed.

Furniture and equipment is often of high quality, because members of such organizations see that as an expression of the value which management puts on them as individuals and co-workers; however, it is not purchased through some procurement function, but in an *ad hoc* way – quite often, in fact, the office holder is allowed to make his or her own choice.

There may be little or no distinction between the quality of the senior and junior managers' working environment. In fact, designer Wally Olins – and design firms are very typical task or person cultures[11] – takes the view that secretaries' desks and chairs ought to be more comfortable than those of the senior executives, because secretarial staff spend more time at them than managers. Olins also stresses the importance of reception areas as indicators of the prevailing culture. How the receptionist treats visitors tends to be a reflection of how staff feel they are viewed by the organization: 'Do they treat you as a human being or as a telephone call incarnate?', he asks.

What is on display there is also a measure of the prevailing culture. Task and person cultures identify heroes, irrespective of their place in the hierarchy, and celebrate their achievements and contributions. Role cultures celebrate the organization and their members' activities (e.g. photographs of who won the annual golf outing) – not necessarily the same thing as achievements in a corporate sense. Power cultures celebrate their leaders. Tom Peters gave an audience in London a telling example of this from his own experience. In the in-flight magazine of an airline company, he noticed a photograph of its chief executive talking to one of the workers. The caption contained a lot of information about the CEO but neither the name nor the function of the worker was mentioned. Peters was not greatly surprised when the airline first lost his luggage, then showed a minimum of interest in recovering it. The company was not showing much interest in its workers. Consequently, they did not care greatly about its customers.

Facilities

The most common sign of the presence of a *power* or *role* culture in British industry is that of separate dining rooms for different layers of management. They are disappearing nowadays but still exist, sometimes in covert forms. A member of one, evidently reluctant, corporate convert to single-staff status described the situation in his office as follows:

The senior managers don't eat in the staff dining rooms much. They go to their clubs or they eat out – there are some restaurants round here that have first class status and frankly a middle manager would get a black mark against them if he or she took a contact there. The price kind of regulates who eats there and also who is entitled to use it for entertainment, though nothing is laid down about that officially. So that cuts right across the single status arrangements that we ostensibly have here. There's also quite a pub culture. Certain groups of managers drink at specific places. If you're not part of their circle, you won't make much progress in their departments.

He made the point that the club culture has the effect of excluding women managers from the social life, and ultimately the career patterns, of those who were headed for the top. In their book on *Tribes*,[12] Desmond Morris and Peter Marsh call areas such as pubs and clubs 'secondary territories' and emphasize their social significance in determining relationships between members of the tribe. But the underlying argument of their book is that the organization has taken the place of the tribe as a social entity.

A related and equally common symbol is the presence of reserved parking spaces. *Task* and *person* cultures share the view expressed by Robert Townsend, author of *Up the organisation*: 'if you're so important, you ought to be there early enough to get a parking space'. An indication of the kind of culture that exists in which parking is on a 'first come, first served' basis is given in Peter Wickens's book about Nissan's management philosophy:[13]

The fact that the managing director has to walk just as far – in the rain – from his parking space to the front door is regarded by many as being important in developing teamworking. The ability to lead does not depend on privilege but on capability in the job. . . .

Breaking the code

Accounts of how codes are cracked by counter-intelligence agencies indicate that once a critical mass of letters and symbols has been deciphered, the rest of the code unravels fairly easily. The same is true of reading corporate cultures. Once one has opened the messages that organizations unwittingly leave around about themselves, a great many other aspects fall into place. One also learns how to look out for and interpret other tell-tale signs. Here are some that are significant in career terms.

Language

Language says a lot about corporate culture, beginning with the wording of job advertisements. Although these are generally drafted by an outside agency, certainly in the case of senior jobs, they are nevertheless approved by the client. In the case of the larger, more experienced executive recruitment intermediaries, it is very likely that the person handling that client's account will try to convey something of his corporate culture in the 'being' description of what the job entails – the personal qualities, as compared to the specific 'doing' skills that it calls for. Thus if the advertisement is heavy on management jargon and stresses reporting responsibilities, it will probably have emanated from a role culture. If it stresses a long string of personal attributes, says recruitment consultant Philip Plumbley, it is probably a self-portrait of how the chairman sees himself: a sure sign of a power culture. We came across what may be a perfect example in *The Sunday Times*. One sentence read:

> The successful candidate will possess personal magnetism, strength of character, drive, determination and all the qualities of a born leader, in addition to being astute and commercially aware.

Some of the significant words which identify different cultures are indicated by Sculley. The contrast between Pepsi, a role culture, and Apple, a task culture, came through in their vocabulary. At Apple, he says,

> ... the conversation was sprinkled with words like 'vision' and 'values' ... They replaced other words in the vocabulary of the

traditional manager, words like 'discipline', 'accountability', 'competition' and 'market wants'.

Internal vocabularies are, in fact, highly significant. The chief executive of a rather staid traditional magazine company, that was taken over by what had originally been a group of advertising salesmen, said that one of the things he noticed was how the vocabulary had changed: they constantly used words such as 'streetwise' and 'street credibility' in discussing courses of action. They also preferred communication to be verbal, rather than written: only financial reports were written. That, he thought, was not only because they were not at home with words, but because it had the effect of depriving subordinates of having any kind of record of their view on policy matters. The culture clash, in this case, eventually proved irreconcilable and the purchasers gave up and sold out to another company.

Another area in which language is highly significant is in sexism. Michael Korda points out that the use of the word 'girls' (usually these days in informal conversation or private memos) instead of 'women' is an infallible indicator of sexist attitudes.

Dress

'By selecting a particular jacket or dress, people make quite specific statements about themselves', Desmond Morris and Peter Marsh write.[14] They point out that although the traditional bowler hat of the English city gent has virtually disappeared from sight, other parts of the uniform – the suit, well polished shoes, sober shirt and club tie – have not. In fact they are now mirrored in the clothes worn by businesswomen, which are really feminizations of menswear in the same business environment.

Person and task cultures, on other hand, tend to be indifferent to such conventions. They will often signal their existence, even in the middle of an alien role culture, by deliberate non-conformism in dress. Suits, for instance, are rarely seen in R & D or design functions. Equally, there are executives who stand out against the prevailing culture by adopting its uniform almost as a parody. The head of a firm of management consultants whom we interviewed, for example, did wear a dark suit, but in combination with an almost dazzling pink tie.

Meeting rooms

Access to meeting rooms is significant. 'Freedom of choice and spontaneity is a real mark of status in power and role cultures', says Dr Steele. In task and person cultures it is the importance of the event that determines access, not the status of the individual.

Another significant piece of evidence, which has been picked up by almost all commentators, relates to the shape of the meeting room table. Square tables are a sign of power and role cultures. A rather sinister account of the aggressive use of a table in a power culture is given in a description of the meeting style of Harold Geneen, the autocrat who built ITT into one of the world's giant conglomerates in the 1960s and 1970s:

> In a locked room high up in the Manhattan headquarters of ITT, executives sit around two long, felt covered tables. There, from all over the world, they are reporting to Geneen ... Geneen's meetings were interrogatory, even adversarial. The use of a microphone [by Geneen] and the formality of the green felt setting amplifed a personal setting into a public spectacle.[15]

The survival rate of cultures such as this in today's corporate climate is not high. ITT's star was on the wane even before Geneen retired. Its critics said it had become what Bob Garrett, in *The learning organisation*,[16] calls a 'brainless business' in which debate is stifled and ideas do not circulate. Indeed, 'no surprises' was Geneen's creed.

The reverse of his approach is seen in organizations in which people at all levels meet and talk freely. Sir John Harvey-Jones describes them well:

> I wanted our executive team to operate as a band of brothers, where discussion was free and uninhibited, where people could get up and walk around, pour themselves a cup of coffee, argue, draw things on flip charts, gesticulate and generally feel easy and unrestricted.

That is the kind of organization which, in career terms, one ought to seek: a place which is developing and which, in doing so, develops one's own career.

Executive summary

Smart moves, as we have said before, are those that align personal values and lifespan development (the subject matters of chapters 4 and 5) with chapter 7's corporate culture: 'the way we do things around here'. Unfortunately, much of that only becomes apparent once you become a member of the organization, whereas it is obviously desirable to anticipate, as far as possible, the behaviour patterns that you are likely to meet. A good summary of these patterns is given in Roger Harrison's famous *Harvard Business Review* article,[17] and is summarized in table 8.1.

A great many clues to corporate culture are there for those who pay attention to the subliminal messages that are communicated by the location, the buildings, the way workspaces are laid out and the look and quality of the furniture and decor.

In looking at a possible career move target, there are a number of things to which it is important to pay attention:

- Discrepancies between what you are told about the organization's values and what you can actually see.
- Cultural indicators: the various kinds of corporate cultures that we described in chapter 7 and the attitudes towards employees and the business environment that these entail are manifested in the 'look of the place'. Power cultures, for instance, have quite a different footprint from person cultures.
- At individual levels, the location of the workplace in relation to peer groups and organization leaders to which you are likely to be assigned says much about the current status of the position.
- The look of the offices and workplaces of the people you meet can also be revealing about their occupants: how they see themselves, the state of their morale, their relationship to others, and how they feel about the organization. It can also indicate the presence of important subcultures which are at odds with the dominant culture of the organization as a whole.

Table 8.1 Interests of people and the organization under four orientations

(a) Interests of people

	Security against economic, political and psychological deprivation	Opportunities for voluntary commitment to worthwhile goals	Opportunities to pursue one's own growth and development independent of organization goals
Power	Low: at the pleasure of the autocrat	Low: unless one is in a sufficiently high position to determine organization goals	Low: unless one is in a sufficiently high position to determine organization goals
Role	High: secured by law, custom and procedure	Low: even if, at times, one is in a high position	Low: organization goals are relatively rigid and activities are closely prescribed
Task	Moderate: psychological deprivation can occur when an individual's contributions are redundant	High: a major basis of the individual's relationship to the organization	Low: the individual should not be in the organization if he or she does not subscribe to some of its goals
Person	High: the individual's welfare is the major concern	High: but only if the individual is capable of generating his or her own goals	High: organization goals are determined by individual needs

(b) Interests of the organization

	Effective response to dangerous, threatening environments	Dealing rapidly and effectively with environmental complexity and change	Internal integration and coordination of effort – if necessary, at the expense of individual needs
Power	High: the organization tends to be perpetually ready for a fight	Moderate to low: depends on size; pyramidal communication channels are easily overloaded	High: effective control emanates from the top
Role	Moderate to low: the organization is slow to mobilize to meet increases in threat	Low: slow to change programmed procedures; communication channels are easily overloaded	High: features a carefully planned rational system of work
Task	Moderate to high: the organization may be slow to make decisions but produces highly competent responses	High: flexible assignment of resources and short communication channels facilitate adaptation	Moderate: integrated by common goal; but flexible, shifting structure may make coordination difficult
Person	Low: the organization is slow to become aware of threat and slow to mobilize effort against it	High: but response is erratic, assignment of resources to problems depends greatly on individual needs and interests	Low: a common goal is difficult to achieve and activities may shift with individual interests

Source: Roger Harrison, 'Understanding your Organization's Character', *Harvard Business Review*, May–June 1972.

Once the importance of these coded messages is understood, others begin to fall into place. Language, dress, the age of most of the people you see around, the number of women in key positions – all are significant. Yet managers who make career moves often distrust these 'soft' inputs as the kind of intuitive response that has no connection with the hard business of management. But they can make all the difference between a smart move and a mismatch.

Notes

1 E. Goffman, *The presentation of self in everyday life* (Penguin, London, 1969/ Anchor, New York, 1959).
2 W. Olins, *The corporate personality* (The Design Council, London, 1978).
3 J. A. Seiler, 'Architecture at work', *Harvard Business Review*, September–October 1984.
4 S. Wilson, *Premises of excellence* (Building Use Studies, London, 1985).
5 'Is Lloyd's fit for the Queen?', *The Independent*, 17 November 1986.
6 Bernard Levin, 'Keeping the commons touch', *The Times*, 7 March 1989.
7 F. Steele, *Making and managing high quality workplaces* (Teachers College Press, New York and London, 1986).
8 M. Korda, *Power! How to get it, how to use it* (Random House, New York/ Weidenfeld & Nicolson, London, 1975).
9 F. Duffy, *Management Today*.
10 A. Furnham, 'Big desks are out, slimline power symbols are in', *The Guardian*.
11 The building occupied by Olins's firm, Wolff Olins, epitomizes its own culture by the fact that what were once closed-off, partitioned floors have been opened up to create a series of open areas flowing into each other.
12 D. Morris and P. Marsh, *Tribes* (Pyramid, London, 1988).
13 P. Wickens, *The road to Nissan* (Macmillan, London, 1988).
14 Morris and Marsh, *Tribes*.
15 R. Pascale and A. Athos, *The art of Japanese management* (Penguin, London, 1986).
16 Bob Garrett, *The learning organisation* (Fontana/Collins, London, 1987).
17 R. Harrison, 'Understanding your organization's character', *Harvard Business Review*, May–June 1972.

9

Rites of Passage

In yet another of his illuminating forays into contemporary anthropology,[1] Desmond Morris, author of *The naked ape*, points to a connection between Boy Scout promises and the agonizing initiation ceremonies undergone by Australian aborigines. He writes, 'Their function is exactly the same, to bind and initiate the young into the lore and customs of the tribe.'

Such rites of passage, he says, are common to all societies when a new member applies for admission to the group. They are also to be found in organizational life: in fact, their first manifestation already occurs in the selection process.

Organizations find selection extraordinarily difficult, because, unlike tribal elders, they know so little about the initiates they are considering – certainly if they come from outside: hence the value and importance that some organizations, especially person cultures such as professional practices and the upper reaches of some financial services firms, attach to networks in their selection processes. These are exhaustively described in Tim Heald's book, *Networks*,[2] which, perhaps significantly, is a work that in Britain is often seen alongside *Who's Who* on the shelves of various kinds of recruitment intermediaries.

Apart from its use in computer jargon, in recent years the term 'network' has come to mean a group of individuals, mainly independent consultants, who informally pool their skills. But, in the sense used by Heald, a network is a group of people who have a 'special relationship' with others from a similar background, or with common interests or experience: school, university, social connections, clubs – even the fact of having worked for the same firm – are all the basis of subsequent networks. Membership of some networks is overtly stated in a CV or is signalled, intention-ally or otherwise, by dress, speech or behaviour. How you look, says Morris, tells a lot about how you want to be seen by others:

> By selecting a particular jacket or dress, people make a quite specific statement about themselves. They declare themselves as individuals, but they simultaneously indicate the extent to which they belong with other sets of individuals.[3]

The reassuring aspect of an identifiable network, from the point of view of an interviewer – and indeed from that of someone being interviewed – is that it is a point of reference, in some cases literally so. In his book, Heald describes how Oliver Lyttleton (Lord Chandos), who was a key figure of several networks (his distinguished career had embraced Eton, Cambridge, sport, the Guards, political office, industry and the Arts – the Lyttleton Theatre is named after him) was in his later years often telephoned to give an opinion on some high-level appointee: 'Chandos would answer "Yes", but whether he approved the appointment, or disapproved, and a hundred and one gradations between, would be conveyed entirely by his inflection.'

In other cases, network membership conveys an expectation, true or otherwise, about training, behaviour or espoused values. For instance, those who have served in the armed forces are generally thought of as disciplined, loyal and reliable; and to have worked for any length of time for a firm such as IBM, Mars or Procter & Gamble is a guarantee of a sound grounding in basic business skills.

Social and economic change have made network membership a much less usable guide. For instance, it is clear from the clothes and accents of some City spokesmen that admission to the higher reaches of at least some financial institutions is now no longer exclusively through the ranks of the old establishment: no use checking the tight little world of who was at Eton, Oxbridge or Harvard with whom. Equally, from the point of view of an indi-vidual career move, one can no longer rely on traditional expecta-tions of what the corporate culture is going to be like. A firm may retain its name, but a change of ownership can change it utterly, as those who have been taken over by Lord Hanson or Mr Maxwell can testify.

Instead of the more or less hard data that comes out of network membership, there is much greater reliance on the vaguer concept of 'personal chemistry' as an initiation test. The significant thing about this is that it is the 'being' rather than the 'doing' aspects that predominate.

Antony Jay tells the story of how he determined, as a junior manager at the BBC, to do away with this highly unscientific approach to selection once he got into the position of being able to make hiring decisions. But in fact he found that when he did get to that stage, one of the first people he had to interview was some-one who was qualified to do the job in every way, except one – he did not actually like him. And so he did not offer him the job. That same point was also made by Henry Ford when he fired Iacocca. 'Well, sometimes you just don't like somebody', was the reason he gave, and it was stronger than the 'doing' attributes that Iacocca had so amply demonstrated as head of the Ford Motor Company.

So who do organizations like? What are the 'being' attributes they look for in the selection part of the initiation process? Edgar Schein puts it very simply: 'Organisations tend to find attractive those candidates who resemble present members in style, assumptions, values and beliefs'.[4] And when it comes to indi-viduals picking other individuals, Jay says that much the same principle applies. He writes, 'Such is the power of the ego that men tend to assume that others of their own kind are, in the end, the best sort of people'.[5]

There are, however, variations of sophistication and openness in the way in which these processes happen. These in turn tell you something about the culture of the organization, and hence whether a move into it would be a good idea. At the crudest level of a power culture, says recruitment consultant Philip Plumbley, the characteristics called for in a job advertisement are a picture of the chief executive as he imagines that he was at the appropriate stage in his career. What appears to be a literal instance of this appeared in an article in *Business*, headed 'Is big bad for Sugar?' In it the marketing director of Apricot Computers is reported as professing surprise at seeing Alan Sugar at a rather low-level trade banquet. He wondered what he was doing there, until he saw several other similar-looking Amstrad employees. 'They all looked like him [i.e. Sugar]', he told the interviewer: 'Burly, with a rough sort of beard'.[6]

At the crudest level a bureaucratic, role culture selection is based on a readiness to conform. That, at any rate, seemed to be the lesson of a 1987 TV documentary on the selection of graduates for the higher ranks of the Civil Service, the so-called Appointments in Administration level. A spikily intelligent young man who had performed well in all the 'doing' tests but who dressed slightly unconventionally and who had worked for a couple of years for the left-oriented Greater London Council was not selected. The choice fell on a young woman with a more conventional set of opinions and who was keen on sport. One was left with the impression that she was felt to be more malleable material than the man. Given her attitudes and background, something could be done with her unformed, and on some issues ill-informed views.

However, also given the fact that Civil Service officials are expected to offer impartial, politically value-free advice to ministers of whatever party is in power, the selection board may not have been all that wrong in applying those criteria. The reason is that it is also probable that a person with strong views of his or her own would sooner or later be running into situations where their own strongly held beliefs and values would come under intolerable pressure to express a value, rather than a technically based opinion – which brings us back to the importance of aligning personal and corporate values in making a career move.

Organizations that have realized this build it quite consciously and systematically into the selection part of the initiation rites. For instance, the big British retailing group, Burton, are in the process of establishing an extremely detailed set of criteria of what personal (being) attributes and doing skills are exhibited by successful Burton managers. The aim is that those conducting interviews will focus their questions around these specific issues. One might say that this merely puts the processes which have been observed by Schein and Jay on a scientific footing; that its managers are really cloning themselves and making it very difficult for anyone coming into their company to introduce change. Against that, Burton's managers argue that a readiness to accept change is one of the criteria in their menu of questions. But certainly anyone thinking of joining an organization that adopts such methods would have to be sure that a willingness to accept change is on the agenda.

The object of such initiation rites is, of course, to find the crock of gold at the end of the selection process rainbow – to predict success. They ask, from an organizational point of view, the question that we suggested in chapter 6 people need to ask themselves: Do you have the right stuff?

Testing, testing

Increasingly, systematic tests of *being* characteristics and *doing* competencies are added to the more subjective measure of personal chemistry in an attempt to establish this, because the cost of making a false move are high, both in organizational and personal terms. As far as the former is concerned, it is generally estimated that, taking all of the factors into account (compensation for loss of office, advertising, fees to intermediaries, disruption in management time) it costs at least two years' pay for the job in question when the person holding it gets fired or leaves. That is why a 1989 survey estimated that the majority of UK firms employing 1000 or more people were using such tests as part of their appointment procedures, internally as well as externally.[7]

The technique that is most often used is that of 'assessment centres'. These are not, as the name might imply, a distinct place to which people are sent to be assessed, but a method of augmenting interviews with a variety of personality and ability tests. Some of these are straightforward responses to written questions and problems. Others are exercises in which a small group of applicants is observed, by managers and psychological consultants, tackling a problem as a team – the objective being to look for those who show the managerial leadership qualities which we described in chapter 6. Another popular test is the so-called 'in-tray' exercise in which you are presented with a pile of unstructured papers, memos and messages relating to some hypothetical organizational problem. You are then given two or three hours to sort out the issues, establish the priorities and come up with a set of recommendations.

In those tests in which the answers are scored, it is not on the conventional pass/fail options of examinations, but on your performance against a norm of scores for the group to which you belong. A financial controller, for instance, would be expected to score highly on questions related to numerical reasoning, but not so highly on verbal expression or on being attributes which are not so strongly related to the role he or she would be undertaking.

Sometimes the norm against which performance in personality tests is measured is that of the values of the organization as well as, or instead of, external criteria such as those of the group to which you belong. That raises the question of whether, if you know the values of the organization very well, it is possible to give answers to personality tests which put you in a favourable light. An amusing appendix to one of the now slightly dated classics of management literature, William H. Whyte's *The organisation man*[8] is entitled 'How to cheat at personality tests' and indicates a number of ways in which this could be done. For instance, he points out that consistency of answers is one of the things testers look out for, so he recommends readers to:

> Strive for the happy mean; on the one hand recognise that a display of too much introversion, a desire for reflection or sensitivity is to be avoided. On the other hand, don't over-compensate. If you try too hard to deny these qualities in yourself, you'll end so far on the other end of the scale as to be rated excessively insensitive or extraverted.

Such advice is always greeted with outrage by occupational psychologists, but the most potent argument against it is neither an ethical nor a scientific one, but to ask whether it serves any purpose to present yourself as being any different from what you are. Sooner or later, the truth will out.

But where does all this leave the 'personal chemistry' of the interview? The answer is that it is still in place. Firstly, assessment centres are very expensive, so they are still mainly used by larger companies, particularly those with a role culture faith in procedures and systems. Secondly, even then interviews still fulfil an important function in confirming and amplifying the objective data from tests. Says recruitment specialist John Courtis, 'They can be used to review and discuss the results of formal tests, are a valid area for exploring communication skills ... they also permit a future boss and employee to decide whether they can tolerate one another'.[9]

Even that, of course, is not unfailingly reliable. John Sculley reports in his book that what made him leave Pepsi for Apple was the charismatic personality of Steve Jobs. 'I was smitten by him', he reports, and the feeling was mutual. But it was not long – and it was probably inevitable – before Jobs's laid back, undisciplined, Californian style clashed with the values of 'the man from corporate America'. The signs of what was to come were already evident in the look of things at Apple. What you see is, as we pointed out in chapter 8, what you get, and it is a crucial part of the total chemistry.

Golden halos

Not all of the initiation is an ordeal. The term 'golden hellos' has entered the language of business to describe the inducements that are sometimes offered to managers to persuade them to jump ship, or to release them from 'golden handcuffs' put on them by their existing employer: for instance, a share option scheme that is triggered by a certain period of service which they will fall short of by leaving. That is not what we mean here, although golden halos and golden hellos sometimes overlap.

What we do mean is that there is a golden halo effect on anyone who joins an organization or who has just been promoted. Its managers or its chief executive also like to feel that they have made a smart move. They have seen all the good reasons for making the appointment and either missed, or not wanted to notice, whatever might be in the shadows. And the feeling is mutual.

Simply from a practical point of view, the best time to make a good deal as well as a smart move is when the decision to appoint you has been made. Reward packages are not the inflexible things they used to be. If there is room for negotiations about conditions, benefits, performance-related bonuses, share option schemes, career development and training opportunities, and all the other items that now take up a substantial part of the total package, that is the time to do it. The question has to be asked: Is the move worth it in these terms – and if not, is there scope for making it so, or more so?

Frankly, some people find it difficult to make such demands in the euphoria and general goodwill that surrounds their appointment to a new role. But looking after one's own interests is an essential part of living in the post-feudal corporate society.

From halos to horns – and back again

One big difference between tribes and organizations is that tribes already know a lot about their initiates by the time they are admitted to full membership. They have seen them grow up and their families are part of the social structure. Organizations used to be like this in the days when it was usual for people to remain with one employer for very long periods, but as we have seen, in the first 15 years of working life, it is now not uncommon for career moves to take place every three years or so.

That leaves initiates vastly ignorant about the informal network of what Deal and Kennedy, the authors of *Corporate cultures*,[10] call 'Spies, storytellers, priests, whisperers, cabals ... the hidden hierarchy which looks considerably different from the organisation chart'.

They came to the conclusion that 'about 90% of what goes on in organisations has nothing to do with formal events'. Their judgement would be confirmed by anyone who has ever worked in an organization, but it does not only apply to what happens at the level of middle management. Sir John Harvey-Jones, writing about the importance of recognizing the informal organization in doing an effective job as chairman – in his case of one of the world's largest companies – comments 'The informal organisation ... is well recognised because unless you have managed to work out how things actually happen, you have no chance of achieving anything at all'.[11]

Harvey-Jones was that now rare phenomenon – a lifetime employee of the company that he eventually came to head. It is clear from his book that knowing the informal as well as the formal hierarchy, and having worked alongside a great many of the senior managers in the company, was a great asset to him when he came to putting together his top team. A lot of commentators also think that the strength of Japanese firms is at least to some extent due to their policy of lifetime employment.[12] This not only means that Japanese managers do not see technological change as a threat to their jobs, but also that they arrive in jobs knowing the ropes and knowing the people they are going to be working with, and vice versa. In other words, they are much more genuinely part of the corporate tribe and can escape some of the messier rituals of initiation.

One advantage of the fact that frequent moves have become a regular part of the career pattern is, however, that the progress of the events that follows a move to another organization – or even another role within an organization – has been charted by a number of intelligent observers. You know what you can expect. We will call these phases encounter, exploration and adjustment/stabilization.

Encounter

In a critical survey of the process of graduate recruitment in Britain,[13] John Moore, a former PA to Lord Sainsbury, found that many of the job market entrants to whom he spoke complained that they were not told enough about what they would actually be doing in the first days at work. But unfamiliarity and bewilderment during this phase is not confined to those entering the job market. It has been recorded right up to chief executive level.

One problem is simply the newness of the surroundings. One does not know where anything is, at what time people generally arrive in the mornings and how the internal communication system works. These are trivial details in themselves, but physical disorientation can be quite upsetting, as witness its use in police and military interrogation.

At the very least, it heightens other stresses which are encountered at quite an early phase, when one discovers that a number of minor things are different. Iacocca mentions that there was a slight stir when he lit up a cigar in his very first meeting with the top brass at Chrysler, and he was somewhat relieved when the chairman announced that he was rescinding forthwith his rule of no smoking at meetings – which was the first Iacocca had heard of its existence. However, he goes on to say, 'before the day was over, I noticed a couple of seemingly insignificant details that gave me pause'. One was the fact that people wandered in and out of the chairman's office at will. The other was that his secretary seemed to be spending a lot of time making personal calls:

> During the first couple of weeks in a new job, you look for tell-tale signs . . . These are the signs I remember and what they told me about Chrysler made me apprehensive about what I was getting into.[14]

John Sculley records similarly disturbing impressions in his first days at Apple. After the tremendous build-up that Steve Jobs had given him about the company, he describes how uneasy he felt about the contrast between the precise, well ordered and disciplined meetings at his previous company, Pepsi, and the noisy shouting matches at Apple, which sometimes degenerated into personal abuse. A report by the PA Consulting Group has highlighted some specific career problems for those who move from what it calls a 'hi-growth company',[15] like Apple, from a more mature one. High growth companies are hectic places, often only one step ahead of chaos. In the words of the report, they work on the basis 'that a constant atmosphere of crisis, where there are never enough people, automatically focusses attention on business priorities.'

Managers coming in from other task-oriented high-growth companies are better at handling this kind of situation than those from big, role-based stable ones. The latter tend to be worried by systems which depend on informal 'know-who' arrangements rather than orderly process. At the same time, it is difficult for them to key into the 'know-who' networks by which things get done because everyone is too busy to show them the ropes.

The result, says the report, is that they then try to make an order they can recognise by focusing on 'all the minor problems which had been ignored up to now simply because they were minor. By changing the focus of their department away from key success factors, they automatically slow down growth.' Such a situation has the makings of the kind of culture clash which is a sure recipe for a false career move.

The shock of first encounters is at least as great at middle management levels. In a privately circulated paper, Bryan Watson, formerly Director of Personnel at what was then one of Britain's largest organizations, the Greater London Council, advocates that there should be 'personal contact between the executive and the new organisation, prior to becoming part of that organisation'.[16] But this hardly ever occurs, and Jean Taylor (not her real name) gave a typical picture of what often happens in the first phase of a new job. She was recruited from a product management post with a leading producer of fast-moving consumer goods to inject marketing expertise into the product design department of an advertising agency:

> It was a new appointment for them and when I met the people I was told I would be working with, we didn't really discuss in any detail what I would be doing. Nobody seemed to have any clear idea of what was involved, but there was a general feeling among the management that they lacked someone with first-hand knowledge of what clients actually wanted – I mean what moves goods off supermarket shelves. The money was fabulous and it was also a chance to move to London where my boy friend was working.
>
> My previous company was very big and pretty conservative. I mean there were rules about most things – written or un-written. There certainly aren't any written rules here. People work as hard as they did where I was before, but it's all rather relaxed. I was a bit taken aback on my very first day when my

secretary didn't come back from lunch until after three. Nobody told me that she'd stayed until after eight the previous Friday to get some urgent work out.

What did throw me, though, was when someone from the creative department came in and asked me to approve some copy for a client's brochure. No one had told me that would be part of my job and I'm not a writer – my degree was in economics. I could see that what she'd done wasn't very good, but I couldn't suggest any specific way of putting it right. I just told her to have another go at it and she got rather shirty when I didn't like her revised draft either. There was a sort of undeclared question that if I couldn't advise her specifically on how to get it right, what exactly could I do?

I suddenly realised that though I'd been introduced as a person, nobody had explained my role. That was going to make it very difficult to do my job.

Exploration

To varying degrees, Jean Taylor's experience was not unusual. 'For the executive joining a new company, the first twelve months are likely to be traumatic', warns Bryan Watson:

> Experience and understanding of the organisational environment and culture assume a high level of importance. This knowledge, which is absorbed rather than learned, is about pecking orders, pressure points, where information is reliable or not, what sort of methods, approaches and ideas succeed in the organisation and which ones fail.

This is particularly difficult for those who move from one kind of culture to another; notably those who move from the public to the private sector, or those whose organizations are merged with another which has different values. A notable instance of that was when, after Big Bang, some of the banks bought up what had previously been stockbroking and venture capital firms. But the whole problem of what can happen when people move from one culture to another was beautifully summed up by President

Truman when he heard he had lost the 1952 US election to General Eisenhower: 'I can't wait for that son of a bitch to come into the White House and find that when he gives an order, nobody obeys it'.

That is also the period in which one has to come to grips with awkward subordinates and difficult superiors. A magazine editor whom we interviewed found that no one had told her before she was appointed that one of her key staff was a crafty and obstructive incompetent who, in his late fifties, was too close to retirement to make it worthwhile firing him. She also found that her finance director was a trusted protégé of the chief executive of the holding company, with the result that a number of changes that she felt were necessary, and which he opposed, could not be implemented. The importance of exact information on the background of the people you will be working with cannot be overemphasized. But unfortunately that knowledge is nearly always gained as part of the exploration process, not before a move is made.

Dr Kurt Einstein, an American management writer, has classified some of the typical initiation rites that may have to be faced during the exploration phase. One is what he calls 'the stranger in paradise', the disorientation to which we have already referred and which has to do with the fact that the physical and culture support systems to which you were previously accustomed are now in a different place. Here are some others:

- *Now let's find out how good you really are*. Instead of easing the new recruit into position, immediate superiors put him or her under pressure with difficult assignments, in order to reassure themselves that they have made the right decision.
- *Not invented here*. Fresh ideas brought in by the new person are rejected on the grounds that he or she 'doesn't understand the business'.
- *The new kid on the block*. This can take two forms. One, suggested by Sir John Harvey-Jones, is that people from the outside are expected by their colleagues, some of whom may have been passed over for the job, 'to perform outstandingly better than any of them could have dreamed of doing'. The other is that

fellow employees may react to protect their territorial rights – and indeed their jobs – against an intruder.

There is also another factor – simple resistance to change. A great many senior management jobs call for someone who can institute or implement change, but existing stakeholders in organizations find change upsetting. There is a natural tendency to seek one's comfort level in any situation. In the context of organizations it is to 'work the system', to find 'quick and dirty' ways of doing one's job quicker, more effectively or with less effort. At the most basic level, a study of how milkmen do their rounds, for instance, showed they often diverged from the route laid down because they found that in that way they could finish work sooner and, in one case, pay an extended call to one house on the route. A middle management change-maker striving to impose his or her own ideas of efficiency would be bound to encounter strong resistance to anything that might change such a routine!

The roots of a deeper psychological resistance to change have been suggested by the American social psychologist Erving Goffman in his influential book, *Asylums*.[17] Although it deals with what happens in closed institutions such as asylums and prisons, what it describes is equally valid for business corporations and their public-sector equivalents. Goffman's argument is that at the point where people become members of an organization they make what he calls a 'primary adjustment' to accepting its corporate culture and the terms of the job description. But, says Goffman, individuals also have an obstinate desire to hang on to their identity, so they then resort to various devices to convince themselves they are still in control of things; for example, choosing to carry out certain tasks their way, rather than in the way that the organization would prefer. Such practices too are attacked by change-makers, but one of the managers we interviewed cautioned against wielding the new broom too vigorously in the exploration period: 'You may be right, but unless you can first build relationships with the stakeholders, you will be alone'.

At a senior level, and particularly when change-making is a key part of the brief, it has been suggested that the best and most successful moves occur when the person appointed to the job is allowed to bring at least one member of his or her team with them to the new assignment. In that way at least there is some kind of support system in place.

Jean Taylor found that her attempts to introduce order and systems were bitterly resented by the creative people: for instance, an attempt to bring in timesheets simply never got off the ground. At the same time she found that she lacked some of the *doing* skills of the job, although in the main these had not been explained to her in the various interviews she had had. 'It think the simple truth was that the management had no clear idea of the job boundaries', she says: 'They knew they had to have someone on board who could see things from the client point of view, but they hadn't thought it through beyond that'.

She was beginning to feel that she would have to force a 'him or me' confrontation with the creative head – which she would almost certainly have lost – when help came from an unexpected quarter. A senior copywriter, a man in his late forties who had, in her words 'a bit of a drink problem' took a liking to her. She was sympathetic because someone in her own family had been an alcoholic. She found that this man was prepared to help her in some of the skill areas where she was deficient. Equally important was that in chatting to him, she gained an insight into the informal office network. For instance her chief antagonist, the creative director, was one of those people with a 'not invented here' complex: 'You had to put ideas to him in a way that made it sound as though he'd thought of them. I found that was a compromise I simply had to make if I wanted to get anything done. But everyone knew that was how he operated, so I did get some credit for introducing new ideas. But I can't say I'm entirely happy with the situation'.

Adjustment and stabilization

Jean Taylor had begun to gain an essential insight into the sub-culture of the organization – the informal events and relationships that account for 90 per cent of the way things actually get done and who you have to influence in order to make it happen. An amusing account of this process, seen from the outside, is given in Gerald Mars's book, *Cheats at work*,[18] in which he describes how office equipment salesmen on a training course are taught to recognize the realities of the power structure when they make a call:

The blockers are those who block access to a sale – people like receptionists. The nose pickers are those who claim to have decision-making powers but really haven't ... W*****s are people who piss around wasting your time. Mr Prospect is a man with executive authority who might actually be prepared to buy. But he might turn into a w***** if a nose picker comes along while you're talking.

This is a somewhat coarse and cynical view, but most people will recognize the truth of its underlying proposition: that the organization chart which is shown to initiates at the interview is not a set of operating instructions when it comes to actually getting anything done. It is only a rough guide, which, during the periods of encounter and exploration, has to be filled with extensive marginal notes about individuals and the characteristics of various functional subcultures. As Mark McCormack says in his bestseller, *What they don't teach you at Harvard Business School,*[19] 'Companies never function according to the organisation chart... the clue is the system. Don't fight it. Use it to find out who the decision makers are, where the shortcuts are'.

It generally turns out that both the physical and human resources are different from what one had expected to find or had been led, usually in all good faith, to believe would be there. In his studies of the initiation process, Kurt Einstein found that one of the marks of a good organization is that it recognizes the difficulties of adjustment that take place by making sure that initiates are given confidence-building tasks that are tough and specific, but achievable. Bad organizations, on the other hand, pressurized initiates by talking of the first six months as a probationary period or openly making it so.

It is important to try and establish which of these attitudes you are likely to find by asking what initial tasks you will be asked to undertake. At the very least, that will force the organization to focus on what specifically needs to be done and what the obstacles are likely to be; the very thing that Jean Taylor's firm had failed to do.

But to reach stability at any level does also call for a readiness to make compromises and adjustments between one's own *being* characteristics and the values of the organization; and between one's own *doing* skills and its resources, both human and physical.

What can happen, though, is that initiates eventually retreat to their own comfort level; opting for an easy life or (and especially in the case of those who have been promoted) going back, in effect if not in title or job description, to doing the job they were doing before. That is related to another, equally fatal mistake: imposing on the organization to which you have moved solutions which worked well before, in another setting and with different people. Successful adjustment, on the other hand, is a learning process which consists of identifying the usable parts of one's previous experience and grafting them on to the best of what is in place. That is how change can be made effective, both in oneself and in its enactment in a new setting:

Jean Taylor is still in two minds about her job, but after eight months her mental balance is tipping in favour of staying on, rather than writing off the move as a mistake. One factor is that another move after such a short period might not look good on her CV. The other is that a recent event has gone a long way to easing the tension on both sides.

'We were in danger of losing a major client – in fact he asked us to make a new pitch for the account', she says: 'If he'd gone elsewhere, the news would have been all over the trade press and everyone knew we would have been under all sorts of pressure. Jobs would probably have been lost'. The presentation involved everyone working flat out for two weeks, including weekends, and it had a successful outcome. Her practical marketing experience proved invaluable in giving shape and direction to the ideas and visuals put together by the creative people. 'Before that, I think we were both inclined to be a bit negative about each other's efforts – to focus on weaknesses rather than putting our strengths together.'

She is still worried about whether her role will have sufficient visibility in the long run. The size of her bonus, she thinks, will reflect the extent to which her contribution is being acknowledged by management. That in turn will influence her decision on the timing of her next move.

Executive summary

The term 'ordeal' is often used by people when they describe the process of joining an organization, or moving to a new setting within it. That word is actually quite appropriate, because what they experience is a modern, corporate version of tribal initiation rites. They are subjected to a number of formal and informal tests to establish their suitability for membership of the tribe.

Traditionally, one of these was to find out whether they belonged to the same network as existing members of the organization, or at least to a similar one. That would establish whether they would be likely to have interests, points of view and values in common. It could also fix literal points of reference to which the existing members of the organization could turn for further information about the initiate.

In a much more fluid social and organizational context, these networks are rather less reliable than they used to be, so the trend is to turn to more scientific methods – primarily psychological tests of aptitude and personality – to back up the notoriously erratic business of interviewing. Nevertheless, interviews are still very important as a way of assessing 'personal chemistry'.

Much of that chemistry really boils down to whether the initiate fits in with the image that the decision-makers have of the organization and of themselves. In the end they tend to appoint people who conform to it. The career lesson is that what you see in these preliminary meetings is what you are going to get if you become a member of the organization.

Moulding yourself into what you are not, by working out how you are supposed to respond in either formal tests or informal interviews, is likely to prove counterproductive, because the prevalent culture will generally prove to be much tougher than the characteristics of an individual who does not fit in with it. A much better move at this stage is to confront some fundamental questions:

- What are the organization's main activities? What are its plans – inasmuch as it is reasonable to disclose them to someone who at this stage is still an outsider? Where is it focusing its investment? Who are its competitors? What and how are they doing?

- What are its human resource policies? Do they promote from inside or outside? Why did the previous incumbent move on? How long was he or she in the job? If you are in the forty plus age group, what is their policy towards older managers? If you are a woman, how many women are there in top jobs?
- What is the background of the decision-makers? Do they come from one dominant function, such as finance or marketing? Is that a background that you share or have an empathy with?
- Does your boss, if you are going to have one, come from the dominant group?
- Who will be your peers? Has anyone been passed over to make room for you?
- Is your role absolutely clear to those who are making the appointment? To those you will be working with? To your immediate subordinates?

The period immediately following acceptance by the organization – and we are talking in days and even hours, rather than weeks – will be the best one in which to secure any changes that you would like to make in the terms and conditions of appointment. This is when goodwill towards the initiate is likely to be at the highest point it will reach for some time thereafter, because of a strong desire by those who have made the appointment to convince themselves that they have made a good decision. After that, the ordeal continues for a period which may last for as long as a year. During this time the initiate goes through various phases which we have described as encounter, exploration and finally, adjustment and stabilization.

During the *encounter* phase the initiate has to find his or her bearings in a new setting, in which the familiar, informal and often subconscious organizational 'handholds' are suddenly absent. In an extreme form, it is like negotiating a room in which one roughly knows where things are – as is the case with a job description – but in which the light has been switched off. The problem is made more acute if the job description turns out to have been inaccurate, as is often the case.

The feeling of bewilderment and, in some degree, disillusionment may be mutual. In the preliminary stages, the initiate will have presented him- or herself in their best light. The encounter phase is also when the organization and its members find out about other aspects, some of which are bound to be less favourable.

This period shades off into one of *exploration*, during which time the initiate begins to get to know the informal organization and its members; how things actually get done and by whom, and where the blocks are. At the same time, he or she may be subjected to a number of informal tests of their competence and resolve. It is important, therefore, that the initial tasks that are set by the organization's managers are clear and achievable, because this is the time when the initiate's credibility is very much at stake.

Reaching the later stages of *stabilization and adjustment* means overcoming the resistance to change – in oneself as well as one's environment. We have suggested that the natural behaviour of organizations and the people in them is to seek a certain 'comfort level' – ways of working the system to their advantage. One of the main reasons why there is resistance to change is that it creates a new set of rules, so that the search for the comfort level has to begin all over again. Resistance to that challenge is an almost universal response, which in the case of the initiate takes the form of retreating to familiar tasks and routines; in effect doing the same job one was doing before, but with a different title ('This is how we did it at XYZ Co.').

That is a defeat. A smart career move, on the other hand, has taken place when the initiate has adapted the best of his or her practice to the best practice that exists in the new setting. The result is a two-way learning process that creates a new kind of energy for both parties.

Notes

1　D. Morris and P. Marsh, *Tribes* (Pyramid, London, 1988).
2　T. Heald, *Networks* (Hodder & Stoughton, London, 1983).
3　Morris and Marsh, *Tribes*.
4　E. Schein, *Organisational culture and leadership* (Jossey Bass, San Francisco, 1985).

5 A. Jay, Management and Machiavelli (Hodder & Stoughton, London, 1967/ Penguin, London, 1970).

6 'Is big bad for Sugar?', Business, July 1989.

7 Personnel Today, 18 April 1989.

8 W. H. Whyte, The organisation man (Simon & Schuster, New York, 1956/ Penguin, London, 1960).

9 J. Courtis, Interviews: skills and strategy (Institute of Personnel Management, London, 1988).

10 T. Deal and A. Kennedy, Corporate cultures: the rites and rituals of corporate life (Penguin, London, 1988).

11 Sir John Harvey-Jones, Making it happen (Collins, London, 1988).

12 J. C. Abbeglen and G. Stalk, Kaisha, the Japanese corporation (Basic Books, New York, 1985).

13 J. Moore, Meeting the challenge of graduate recruitment (unpublished paper, The Harwood Company, London, 1989).

14 L. Iacocca, Iacocca, an autobiography (Bantam, New York, 1984).

15 Managing the Hi-Growth Company. PA Consulting Group, 1990, London.

16 B. Watson, Executive mobility and effectiveness (unpublished paper, London, 1988).

17 E. Goffman, Asylums (Doubleday, New York, 1961).

18 G. Mars, Cheats at work, the anthropology of the workplace (Counterpoint, London, 1983).

19 M. McCormack, What they don't teach you at Harvard Business School (Fontana/Collins, London, 1986).

10

Paths up the Pyramid

Not long ago, on a business trip to Scandinavia, one of us engaged in conversation after dinner in the bar of an Oslo hotel with an interesting, youngish-looking British fellow guest. He was, perhaps, in his early forties and said that he was in the armed forces. Apart from that he was not very forthcoming about what he did, although he said that he had been a pilot at one time and was now in 'more of a desk job'. At breakfast the next morning he appeared in uniform – that of an air vice-marshal, the equivalent of a two-star general.

Apart from the personal shock of having reached an age at which not merely policemen but even senior officers look young, the incident illustrated a salient point about careers: those who are on a fast track get to or near the top at a fairly early age. In civilian life, the experience of headhunters is that potential chief executives will be close to a main board appointment by their mid-to-late thirties and will have served on the board of a subsidiary before then. The majority of the high-flyers interviewed by Charles Cox and Cary Cooper[1] had had early and successful experiences of management, characteristically in a role with considerable visibility – managing a turnaround or running an overseas subsidiary. The question is: Can you plan for such opportunities or are they a matter of luck?

Again, most of the people who Cox and Cooper talked to put their progress down to being in the right place at the right time, and that was also confirmed by the people we interviewed. But when we dug a little deeper, their version of what constituted luck came close to the memorable statement once made by the golfer, Gary Player: 'The more I practice, the luckier I get'. In the context that we are discussing, luck turned out to be an ability to recognize and capitalize on opportunities, allied to a sense of timing of when to move and when to stick.

What they notably did *not* have was a hard and fast plan for a set of moves related to a fixed goal, such as being chief executive of a major company by the time they were 45. Oddly enough, this was the declared objective of some MBA students in a recent career seminar at Harvard Business School, but one would guess that those who saw their career in those terms would be unlikely to get there. This is because realistic career plans have to take account not only of the instability of the external environment – which raises the question of how useful even a blue chip MBA might be in 15 years' time – but also of changes in one's own attitudes and circumstances and discoveries about one's being attributes and doing skills.

However, that does not mean that careers develop purely opportunistically without an underlying theme; an ambition to move broadly in a certain course and to follow, again broadly, a certain view of oneself in the future. As one very successful young executive put it, relating his own career path to early childhood influences: 'I was always expected to get on and do well'.

That is a pretty general brief, but it comes close to the kind of career plan that successful managers have. It involves trying a variety of roles to see which one best fits doing, being and the alignment of those things with various corporate cultures.

A good analogy with this perhaps abstract-seeming concept is given by an American consultant, Professor Andrew Souerwine, in his book, *Career strategies*.[2] He talks of careers being driven by an underlying purpose. Let us assume, he says, that it is simply making money. He advises readers to list various ways of doing that, which could include asking for a raise, changing jobs, playing the stock market, starting a business on the side and so forth:

Note that in all these cases, the purpose remains clear: to make more money. The roles, however, change ... And as the roles change, the individuals planning them display varying levels of discomfort, depending on their own value systems.

So how far ahead can you plan to try a variety of roles for size? The view expressed by Stephen Rowlinson, formerly UK chief of the big headhunting firm, Korn Ferry, is that five years is about as far as you can reasonably look ahead.[3] The pattern that head-hunters look for over such a period is a series of moves which involve adding new skills and trying new roles within the context of a broad career aim. It is this last factor which distinguishes potential high-flyers from job-hoppers.

In fact, the whole process is very similar, both in content and in the length of time it covers, to a business plan. Although we are cautious about offering quick fixes and prescriptive solutions, we would like to suggest drawing up such a plan for yourself. Without that it is impossible to articulate your own aspirations and – equally important – to articulate them to others. As one of the top MDs interviewed by Cox and Cooper puts it: 'I think one of the biggest problems I have is to persuade people to tell me their aspirations. If you want to get into the main line of business, you had better say so.

Business plans and career equivalents

Business objectives over a 3–5 year period   Career objectives: where you would like to be in 3–5 years time, in terms of function, level, industry, location, people you want to work with and the kind of experience you want to obtain. Goals are neither abstract nor absolute, but related to individual needs and, in broad terms, aspirations.

Business history   Career progression so far, patterns of achievement and personal satisfaction. Do these indicate that your objectives are realistic?

The background of the management team   Personal experience, respon-sibilities and where you need further development to reach your goals, either through formal training or additional experience.

The market for the business   The anticipated state of the job market over 3–5 years for existing personal skills, qualifications and experience by function, type of business and geographical area. Are there any economic or technical changes emerging which might affect things positively or otherwise?

Products   What are the *doing* and *being* 'products' that you have to offer? Will they meet market needs over a 3–5 year period? What adaptation, training and further development is required? What products do you definitely not have that are also beyond your reach, for example verbal or numerical skills of a higher order, or career anchors that are very firmly set? Do these factors matter in relation to your objectives?

Pricing   What are your reward aims and needs? Are they realistic? How flexible can you afford to be?

Suppliers   Can these various objectives of material reward, career development and broad personal ambition be met by existing 'suppliers' – in this case current employers and/or other providers of job opportunities? What specific action needs to be taken to ensure that suppliers are in place and able to deliver? You may end up being your own supplier – self-employed, running your own business.

Physical resources   Do you have what it takes, in terms of physical health and psychological stamina, to reach the objectives you have set yourself? Do you have the financial resources for self-employment or self-development; for example, can you take a year off to do an MBA? Or are you enough of a sticker to do it part-time?

Contingency plans   Do you have a viable, personally satisfactory fall-back position, if you cannot reach your first objectives or cannot get the tools to do so? Particularly in the later stages of a career, it is important to have other things you can do, options and interests that can be developed.

Avoiding the straight and narrow

Cox and Cooper found that although the backgrounds, attitudes and working methods of their high-flyers were very diverse, there were a few elements in common. One of these was that most of them had moved around a great deal, especially in the first years of their careers. Our discussions with successful managers confirmed that. Here, for instance, are just a few of their very diverse career experiences:

- From graduate trainee at Courtauld to market development executive in financial services. From there to product manager in a toy company. Then to marketing manager in a household goods and toiletries firm, going on to director level roles in retail merchandizing. Now (at 38) trading director of a major PLC food company.
- From research biochemist into marketing. Then selling up every realizable asset that she had to buy into the equity of a small design company. Became chief executive by the time she was 35. Her company is now amongst the top ten in the UK.
- From Merchant Navy cadet to (at 22) management trainee, to (at 24) personal assistant to the President of one of the US's largest companies. From there to line management in a number of expatriate locations and then, from 35 on, to a variety of headquarters positions at CEO level – each move to a company of greater importance than the last. At 47, headhunted to become CEO of one of Britain's largest firms.
- From university lecturer (in Paris) to the personal staff of an MP. From there to a government agency and then into industry as secretary to the board of a major PLC. Then to a board appointment, first with that company and then, at 36, to a much larger one. Now in charge of one of its main divisions – a £10 billion a year business.
- From a civil-service-type administrative job with an employers' organization to running one of its regional offices. Back to one of its top headquarters jobs, then into industry on the board of a company headed by one of the UK's most high-profile chief executives. At 42, felt he had reached his peak there. Moved into one of the key jobs in a major public-sector organization. Now chief executive of one of Britain's largest firms.
- Within one company (IBM, UK), from sales and marketing to training. Then becoming an expert in a very esoteric software

development and going on to run an 'intrapreneuring' venture in the company – in effect pioneering a diversification venture.

One of the senior managers in this group summed up what would be a typical view of career moves. He had, he said, made several moves in his twenties, and although they appeared to be in a variety of fairly unrelated industries and roles, there was a common theme. It was not money. Each one, he said, expanded his knowledge and his range of experience. Each one challenged him intellectually, and when he felt that he had reached the point at which the job's possibilities were becoming too narrowly focused, he moved on. His career only started to stabilize in his early thirties, when he began to form a clearer picture of what drove him and others.

Most recruiters agree on the value of making quite frequent job changes in the early stages of your career. After that opinions differ. Nicholson and West's study of mobility patterns in management[4] indicated that 'the upward status moves people make between organisations are larger vertical steps than the upward status moves they make within organisations'. In other words, if you want to move up fast, you should do so by changing employers as well as functions. On the other hand, this seems to be mainly true of careers in smaller organizations. It also seems to be the case that specialists are more ready to make frequent moves than are generalists: they found that 'the most radical moves may be undertaken by people with the greatest confidence in the transferability of their skills'.

This implies that generalists in larger companies might best advance their careers, if not by staying put, then at least by staying longer – but also by changing functions while doing so. That, coupled with a consistent record of achievement, is the career pattern which headhunters like to see once managers become senior enough to come into their sights. This is because of the very widespread view that the structure of organizations is changing. 'Organisations used to look like a collection of ladders tied together at the top', says Professor Charles Handy in *The age of unreason*:[5] 'A career for most people meant climbing the ladder'. In the new organization, he says, there will be far fewer rungs –

perhaps as few as in universities, where there are only three grades below full professor. So fast-track careers are, as is already the case in some Japanese firms, 'a horizontal fast track, a succession of different jobs, real jobs with tough standards to be met, but all at the same level'.

A capacity to see career-enhancing lateral opportunities is now more important than having your eyes fixed on the next rung up. For instance, the human resource director of one very large UK firm, who started working life as a physicist, has held jobs at a similar level in its research and development, marketing and finance functions. That process has not only been one of personal development, but a course which, when he gets to the top, will mean that he arrives equipped with a vast amount of knowledge and experience about people, functions and the extent of his own skills and competencies. A survey produced by the headhunting firm Korn Ferry identifies what it regards as the classic career moves for high-flyers:[6]

- Marketing, because it involves a cross-section of customers, competitors, product design and cost structure. This includes most of the factors that have a bearing on management decisions.
- Corporate finance, because of the strategic role of disposals, mergers and acquisitions.
- Experience in human resource management, because people rather than plants are the assets of knowledge-based organizations.
- A track record in turnarounds and in overseas assignments.

However, headhunters warn those looking for big-company careers that this kind of career track can only be experienced within an organization. In that sphere, it is virtually impossible to make lateral functional moves from outside to inside. For instance, a finance director would find it extremely difficult to make a move into general management, unless he did so within his own firm. That is a strong argument for those with general management ambitions in large companies to stick with them once they pass thirtysomething.

Working abroad

A crucial step in the career course of those who see themselves as high-flyers is, as we have said earlier, to obtain leadership experience. 'There's no substitute for experiencing command', a deputy chief constable told Professor Kakabadse in his study of career patterns in the police: 'It is the personal experience of command that makes you or breaks you'.[7]

One of the standard ways of gaining that experience is proving to be a spell of working abroad. Nearly all of Cox and Cooper's high-flyers had done that, and the increasing globalization of world trade is bound to increase the trend. But what is accepted as sound practice and what happens in reality are not necessarily the same thing. There are still organizations in which, intentionally or otherwise, being sent abroad is a trip to a career Siberia rather than a stop-off on the way to the promised land. Here are some indicators about which is which:

- *Pre-assignment briefing for all concerned – including the spouse.* If there is little corporate effort being put into that, the chances are that a spell abroad is not rated highly.
- *A logical reward structure.* This should consist of a core salary equivalent to 'the rate for the job' at home, plus an international location allowance which reflects differences in the cost of living. Plucking a figure out of the air, even if it is a temptingly large one, shows that the organization has no real plan for integrating expatriate experience.
- *Proper mechanisms for keeping in touch with home base.* Home visits should be more than just holidays. For example, at Barclays Bank 'all expatriates who come home on leave must make themselves available for at least two days of head office interviews'.[8] Performance appraisals should be part of that process. There should also be visits to the location by senior executives from the home company and organized channels of communication generally. An 'out of sight, out of mind' policy is a bad sign, even if it is unintentional.
- *Pre-return planning.* If a posting abroad is taken seriously as an aspect of career development, financial, logistic and career

aspects should all be discussed with expatriate managers about six months before the assignment ends. On returning home, the expatriate's experience should be used intelligently; for instance, by attaching him or her to a task force developing aspects of the organization's policy in the relevant locations.

• *Subsequent careers of expatriates.* Where are they now? If they have sunk without trace or left the organization, it might be better to start looking for another job rather than taking a step into exile.

The good boss guide

The experience of having worked in close association with a powerful boss ranks alongside that of working abroad as a theme in the career track of high-flyers. But although there are dozens of books and innumerable articles on the art of managing subordinates, the literature on the advice of managing upward relationships is rather sparse. Yet this skill is vital in two respects.

Firstly, as Professor Kakabadse found from the senior police officers he interviewed, being able to influence effectively in circumstances where one cannot command is an essential aspect of learning to be a manager. Secondly, as the American writer Rosabeth Moss Kanter reports, credibility with superiors also makes managers more effective with subordinates.[9]

Relationships with a powerful boss tend to have an admiration-hate quality. A good account, which was also roughly similar to the story we heard from others about such associations, was given by one of the people we interviewed. Now himself head of a large company, he described an earlier part of his career when he worked directly under one of Britain's best known and toughest chief executives:

Let me say right away, I learned a tremendous lot from him and from the experience of working for him. He challenged you all the time. You had to defend everything in bottom line terms. That was the only vision that counted with him, but it worked because it was absolutely, unequivocally clear. If you could make a case for something in those terms – and you'd have to argue it closely and clearly – he would let you get on with it. But not until you'd convinced him.

The process of defending yourself constantly wore some people out. Ultimately they tended to become functionaries, psychologically subordinated and dependent on the boss in a curious way – rather like the way kidnap victims form a relationship with their kidnapper. When I felt just a hint of that in my own attitudes, I decided it was time to move on, even though I was on the main board and by then fairly well known nationally in my industry.

The relationship he was describing was characteristic of that which develops between boss and subordinate in a cross between a power and a role culture. Indeed, such associations generally reflect the types of corporate culture we described in chapters 7 and 8. At one extreme there are power and role cultures in which subordinates play the part of 'gofers' and are bound by procedures, rules about the way things are done and by organizational hierarchies. At the other end there are task and person cultures, in which what the boss values are ideas, ways of developing human resources, the flow of communications, and the speed and quality of response to the market.

None of these approaches to managing organizations is 'the answer'. They all have strengths and weaknesses. For instance, the divergent thinkers who tend to head up task and person cultures are good listeners and are open to ideas but sometimes find it difficult to make up their minds between the options on offer. The enthusiasts who run some first-generation power cultures have a tendency to rush off on impulse in pursuit of an idea that is often as likely to break them as make them. On the other hand, the balanced, logical bosses who are often found in role cultures are apt to err on the side of caution.

There is no added value when subordinates merely clone the boss. That is why corporate history is full of loyal number twos who, when it came to their turn, failed to become or to make a success of being number one. But fighting the boss is not the answer either. Bosses are not immune to seeing change as a threat and both parties, bosses and subordinates, instinctively view their relationship as something of a power struggle. But it is also a mistake to regard it as a zero-sum game, in which there is a winner and a loser. In that case, the odds are that the subordinate will be the one who loses. The secret is to find a balance of what one commentator calls 'a workable set of mutual expectations'.[10]

To arrive at that, there are some simple approaches that subordinates can take – without becoming or being perceived as either their master's voice or their master's adversary:

- *Put forward alternatives*. No one likes to be presented with a 'do this, or else' option. It is less likely to produce a decision than offering two or three well argued possible courses of action. That also indicates that you yourself have considered the alternatives.
- *Minimize the penalties for failure*. Rather than recommending ambitious, expensive courses of action, many bosses prefer projects which try things out, where likely results can be discerned quickly and which can be abandoned without publicity, loss of face and heavy costs if they do not work out.
- *Make sure the boss also gets credit for something the subordinate has done*. If you grab all the credit yourself you are laying up a store of hostility for the future.
- *Fit in with the boss's preferred method of working*. Does he or she react best to long, detailed presentations or to short memos? Does he or she prefer one to one argument or consensus with the whole top team – in which case you will have to make sure your allies are in place?

Those are just a few of many factors that repay study in the way you approach the boss–subordinate relationship. Barry Curnow, the head of the big human resource consultancy MSL, even suggests looking up the boss in *Who's who*. Those with solitary pursuits, he says, may be remote loners who are difficult to work with.

There is, in fact, a demonology of bosses, described by Professor Kets de Vries of INSEAD, a management consultant and academic who is also a psychoanalyst. In an article entitled 'Managers who drive their companies mad' he suggests that organizations suffer from neuroses which are a product of those of their bosses.[11] For instance, there are depressive companies in which nothing happens, compulsive ones in which every small detail has to be settled before anything is undertaken, and schizoid ones in which, because the leader is weak, more effort is spent on in-fighting than anything else. Since it is no part of a subordinate's job to be a therapist, such situations should be avoided if your role is to be that of a subordinate.

Being visible

'Being stretched by an immediate boss' was one of the important career development factors cited by the senior police officers interviewed by Andrew Kakabadse and Paul Dainty: the other was 'becoming visible to top management before the age of 30'. These are themes that recur in talking to managers in organizations of all kinds.

In fact, the concept of visibility, which we also touched on in chapter 1, is important over the entire upward curve of a career. As Rosabeth Moss Kanter found in her study of an organization from the inside,[12] 'People who looked like "comers" seemed to have an instinct for doing the visible'. For instance, a marketing manager discovered that there was a communication gap about the activities in that department, so he sent round a weekly report of what his department was doing. As well as being useful, that immediately put him on the organizational map.[13]

The opportunities for doing visible things also vary and are to some extent determined by the corporate culture. In an earlier chapter we asked the rhetorical question, 'Whoever heard of anyone at Body Shop, other than Anita and Gordon Roddick?' It illustrates the difficulty that outsiders face in an entrepreneurial power culture, yet even here there are opportunities. A lot of entrepreneurs, for instance, are bored by implementation and there is scope for people who are natural implementers to make themselves visible. The chief executive we interviewed above, to take another case, found that his boss did not like making public appearances, and was happy to leave it to him to take the highly visible role of company spokesman when the media wanted to report someone in the company at top level. Jobs that 'straddle the boundaries between the organisation and its environment tend to be more noticeable', says Kanter.[14]

The big problem with visibility, headhunters say, is in person cultures such as consultancies, because so much of what they do is a team effort. Ideas, for instance, often come from the team and are brainstormed in ways which make it difficult for individuals to emerge in any highly visible way.

Role cultures pose another set of obstacles. An hierarchical system, says Antony Jay in *Management and Machiavelli*,[15] enshrines and sanctifies the qualities that brought success in the past and continues to search for and promote those who possess similar attributes. Michael Korda in *Power*[16] also makes the point that, in such organizations, moving up the ladder depends on someone else moving or falling off it. The only way you can achieve visibility is to expand your function, by empire building.

Looking strategically at moves to enhance visibility, such cultures are generally regarded as ones to avoid, certainly in earlier stages of a career. They are the slow-moving mastodons that are most vulnerable to predators. The organizations of the future are the fast-moving, project-oriented task cultures. It is here where people work in flat pyramids and are given opportunities to make their mark, irrespective of age or status. On the other hand, it is important to distinguish between organizations that are big and strong and those that are merely fat and sluggish. Some big, well managed, good role culture organizations are also prime territory for headhunters because they have a reputation for being choosey about who they take on, and you have to be good to be hired. Indeed, an article in *The Economist*[17] on 'Britain's most admired companies' makes the point that such firms are 'an obligatory first stop for headhunters', which makes them very anxious to create career structures that enable them to retain their brightest managers. But in such settings you also have to be careful to find visible settings. As we pointed out in chapter 2, it is better, for instance, to be involved in their new products than with established brands, where the best you can do is to increase the market share by a percentage point or two.

Women and visibility

Women have one inherent advantage in the matter of visibility. Except for those who have started their own businesses, there are, as yet, so few of them in senior management that their mere presence in executive roles is bound to be noticed. In 1988 there were only eight women among the approximately 1000 directors of the top 100 British companies, although women account for almost 45 per cent of the total workforce.[18] The imbalance between numbers and status in many other industrialized Western countries is similar, and it is very much worse in Japan and the Far East.

The situation is bound to change because of demographic factors and the growth of women's influence in politics, but men will not readily make way for women above the 'glass ceiling' level of middle management. A classic ploy to limit female visibility is to confine them to specialist staff functions when the career curve of those who aspire to general management jobs has, at some point, to run through line experience. A woman engineer reports, for instance, that she had to fight for a 'hard hat' job on site in a company which, though it paid lip service to the need for women, then restricted them to staff roles which carried only very limited career scope and had a relatively low status.

Her experience illustrates two points that were made to us by women managers. One was that women have to fight for visibility over territory that men take for granted. A very senior manager recounted how she at first had to *ask* to be included in after-work social occasions with executives of client companies with whom she and her male colleagues were dealing during the day.

The other problem was that of 'tokenism', being the 'token woman' in a male-dominated environment. Token women generally find that they are kept out of the male network in which the big decisions are made, often as the result of informal discussions. 'A lot of male managers find it difficult to talk to women in the same unguarded way as they talk to their colleagues', one woman manager commented. She chose the company that she eventually joined because it had a high proportion of women in top jobs and a 25 per cent representation on the main board.

She went there in preference to another company where she was interviewed by men she found 'nice, but a bit fatherly, a bit patronising'. Further open and covert signs of male-dominated cultures are charted by Michael Korda in his book, *Male chauvinism*.[19] Although it was published in the early 1970s, much of what he says about warning signs for women still holds true:

- *Organizations which tend to group women executives together.* 'By isolating them', he writes of one such place, 'it became possible to treat them as a group, like secretaries, instead of as individually successful executives.'
- *Organizations in which women's success is defined by job or salary:* for example, where statements are made such as 'a successful woman can make £35,000 a year here'. Despite legislation, many organizations in the private sector still find ways of paying less to women than to men. In such organizations, Korda writes, 'Men behave as if money were a kind of masculine special concern, as if every man were a potential husband and father of three children, even when he's a bachelor, and every woman were being supported by someone'.
- *Organizations which (usually unconsciously) use sexist language.* 'Men frequently say "office" as a euphemism for "secretary"', says Michael Korda. Another typical example of sexist terminology is what he calls 'meaningless upgrading' for the benefit of women colleagues: referring to a secretary as 'my assistant', but only when women are present.

Private-sector role cultures are those in which such attitudes are most prevalent and in which it is hardest for women to achieve visibility. In power cultures, it depends somewhat on the chief executive: Korda suggests that CEOs with daughters who are developing their own careers are likely to be sympathetic to the claims of women executives. In another such organization, in which there is a strong family atmosphere, the role of women was also naturally accepted.

However, it is in person and task cultures, such as professional practices and the new 'sunrise' industries, where women managers have made the greatest impact and where there is a

critical mass of supportive women managers. In such organizations, women's style of working – getting things done through
networks and collaboration across functional boundaries and
disciplines – is proving to be particularly effective. The article on
women's careers in the *New York Times* to which we have already
referred describes this as the implementation of 'new generation
values'. It says that research shows that a third of managers (of
both sexes) under 30 espouse those values, rather than the
adversarial methods of traditional management which men are
perhaps better at using.

The big problem for women, though, is that the battle for
visibility often has to be fought on two fronts; at home, or to be
more precise, in their private lives, as well as in the office. In the
early part of their careers, the conflict is between that and an
active social life. A successful woman manager in her late thirties
met the man she eventually married while still at university. She
thought that forming a stable relationship early was important for
career-minded women, since it became increasingly more difficult
for them to meet people, except through work.

She and her husband both earned fairly large salaries, which
made it possible for them to afford a nanny and other domestic
help. For couples not so well placed, the problem is, as one
woman put it, that 'very few men are liberated when it comes to
housework', which means that many women's careers come to at
least a temporary halt when they decide to have children. That is
something women have to take into account when establishing
relationships. An article about dual-career couples in Germany
showed that only 8 per cent of men took their partner's career
into account when planning their future.[20] That is probably
characteristic of other countries as well.

The real challenge comes when a choice has to be made about
whose career will predominate. That is particularly likely to come
to a head when one partner has to make a career move to a job
abroad. As we said earlier, this is a common step for high-flyers.
An article in *The Times*, headed 'Going to work on a weekend
marriage',[21] suggests that 'commuter marriages' in which the
partners only spend weekends together might not be very different from arrangements in which they hardly see each other during

the week anyway. But another decision is whether such sacrifices are worth it. It is worth noting the *New York Times*'s comments on the issue. In new-generation organizations, it says,

> The most effective managers are not single minded careerists willing to sacrifice personal life to climb the corporate ladder ... they temper their passion to win with an understanding heart.

The importance of being earnest about learning

Training, as Professor Handy has pointed out, used to be regarded by managers almost as a punishment, a signal that they were considered not to be quite up to scratch in some aspect of their job. Now it is being seen as a reward or incentive and a sign that they are being groomed for higher things. This is because of the recognition, tacit or otherwise, that in an information-based, post-feudal workplace, the level and up-to-dateness of one's knowledge is the most tradeable asset one has. In terms of employability it is the universal tool in anyone's career management kit. As Rosabeth Moss Kanter observes, 'If security no longer comes from being employed, then it must come from being employable'.[22]

For many managers the most prized form of training is an MBA. The number of people taking MBA courses in the UK has risen dramatically in the past five years and is continuing to do so, through one of several options:

- The in-company MBA, in which the course content is closely linked to specific company needs, even though it is designed and administered by a university or polytechnic. The criticism of this option is that it is too inward-looking and that it lacks the stimulus of 'a cross section of managers from different backgrounds which is found on a traditional open programme'.[23]
- The consortium MBA, in which several organizations club together to specify their needs and then invite a polytechnic to

design the course. This gets round the problem of the MBA being too linked to a single company, culture and enrolment.

- The company-sponsored MBA, where the employer simply pays for an employee to take a full-time or distance learning course at one of the business schools. This option is now not so popular with employers, because such MBAs, not being company-specific, are very transferable to competitors cashing in on another company's investment in training.
- Self-funded MBAs, taken either by distance learning or through a full-time career break.

For the individual, all of these options involve a considerable commitment in time, and the self-funding option also calls for a purely financial investment in one's future of anything between £10 000 and £20 000. But is an MBA worth it as a career move?

To some extent the answer depends on the institution awarding the degree. In Europe the alumni of schools such as London, Cranfield, Manchester, INSEAD in France and IMEDE in Switzerland are highly regarded by employers. Then there are schools which have a good reputation in one particular department or speciality; and some are seen, rightly or wrongly, as second-division players.

The rest of the answer is concerned with personal objectives. One of these is obviously money. Financial services and management consultancy firms are prepared to pay a premium to attract MBAs, in particular the alumni of the blue riband schools. In other industries, the possession of an MBA may be a bargaining point, but not a decisive advantage.

In entrepreneurially led power cultures the MBA tends not to cut much ice at all. Their view is that quoted by Cox and Cooper: 'High flyers get on and do things. They do not spend time on training programmes'. Role cultures, particularly the more decadent ones, echo this line. Here MBAs are often spoken of as academic-theory-soaked know-it-alls.

The other reason why people take an MBA is to enable them to make smart career moves, but headhunters have some trenchant views on this:

- Taking an MBA to make a move out of a speciality or a staff role in one organization into senior line management in another is a misguided notion, although it might facilitate an upward-spiralling intra-company move.
- As the MBA becomes less rare, it is important to remember that when you move back into the job market, you are competing for position with people who have both practical experience *and* an MBA.
- MBAs are most highly rewarded in financial services and consultancy. The common tendency is for new MBA graduates to head for this sector to recoup quickly their money and time investment, with the intention of transferring into line management later. But such moves are extremely difficult to make because consultancy or financial services experience and skills are regarded as being radically different from those required by line managers.
- An MBA, like any other qualification, has a shelf life. Its significance in the eyes of headhunters is lessened by the passage of time in favour of where one is and how one has got there.

However, training takes many forms other than studying for an MBA. In 1988 the total expenditure on management training in the UK was estimated to be £250 m and in Europe £1.6 bn overall.[24] But there are training courses which are genuinely career-enhancing and those which merely pay lip service to the notion by sending managers off to be instructed in the topic that is 'flavour of the month'. Organizations which have a real commitment to training are termed 'learning organizations'. They are the ones in which learning is a continuous process, which has genuine top-down sponsorship and which is constantly updated and transferred from the individual to the organization as an instrument of change. The characteristics of such organizations are identified in an excellent monograph produced by Ashridge Management College[25] and include the following key features:

- Training and development is a continuous process and is an integral part of corporate strategy – an investment, not a cost.

- Specialist training courses are available across the knowledge, skill and value spectrum. They are linked to individual as well as corporate goals or needs, and are monitored and altered in the light of experience.
- There is self-selection for training. In one US plant, often cited by Tom Peters, any employee, at any level, can obtain training in any topic at company expense.
- Failure is tolerated as part of the learning process. In one of the world's great learning organizations, IBM, one of the significant corporate legends concerns a young manager who made a mistake which cost the company $10 m. 'I suppose you're going to fire me?' he asked when summoned by IBM's chief executive, Tom Watson Jr: to which Watson is supposed to have replied, 'Fire you? Hell no – we just spent ten millions bucks training you'.

Executive summary

Most people who are headed for the top start making their presence felt early: former Royal Navy man Harvey-Jones puts it neatly in saying that you can see future First Sea Lords a long way off. In civilian life you have to have had significant management experience and be close to a major board appointment, or its public-sector equivalent, by your mid- to late thirties if you are going to make it at all.

But to what extent can the moves leading up to that point be planned? Being in the right place in the right time is often cited by successful managers as part of the secret, but on closer examination it turns out they *make* their luck by a mixture of ability to maximize their opportunities, plus a sure instinct for knowing when to move and when to stick in the context of a broad career agenda. This can be set out as a business plan, which looks ahead for a similar length of time – about three years.

It does not, however, represent the map of a straight path up the organization. Ideally, it should expose one to a wide range of high-quality experience in marketing, finance, human resource management and working overseas. But, in the opinion of headhunters, it is difficult to climb that zig-zag path by switching mountains to gain height. Within his or her organization a high-flying human resource manager (to take a case in point) might well be rotated to other functions; but it would be virtually impossible for them to be taken on by another large organization in a different role. That is a strong argument for career stability in the crucial thirtysomething years.

A key part of that experience, particularly in relation to the development of *being* attributes, is working with a boss who 'stretches' you. Apart from the benefits, in terms of management development, of sitting alongside a 'pro', it teaches you to work in and adapt yourself to situations which you cannot fully control. The lessons of such a relationship are neither to clone the boss nor to fight him or her, but to find ways of complementing them and to learn to sell your ideas persuasively.

There are, however, some bosses to be avoided – amongst them the ones that deny their subordinates the oxygen of visibility. Visibility is essential for those who aspire to senior management, but it is difficult to achieve in an entrepreneurial power culture – the boss is usually the one who is credited with activities from which visibility derives. It is also difficult to achieve in some types of person cultures, notably consultancies, where a good deal of what happens is a team effort. By contrast, well managed role cultures are quite good at providing visibility because of the importance they attach to training, management development and even selection. There are firms that are known to hire only good people. Task cultures are also a good place in which to be visible, because of their emphasis on project and taskforce work. Credit visibly attaches to successful managers in such firms.

Visibility can be a problem for women managers because so many cultures are male-dominated. Often they have to fight for it, by ensuring that they are not marginalized, intentionally or other-wise, into non-visible roles. As things stand at present, their best plan may be to make career moves into organizations in which women have more than a token presence – and to avoid organiza-tions in which sexism is the sin that dares not speak its name.

Task and person cultures, because of the way they work across functions and through skill-based teams, are most likely to be woman-friendly, and there is a growing number of woman managers in such fields as law, accountancy and financial services. But women have to fight for visibility on two fronts and to reconcile traditional domestic role assumptions with a career. It is partly the responsibility of organizations to create a climate which enables them to do that; but it is also a matter of sorting out personal relationships and priorities.

Training is another vital part of career development. Doing an MBA has been seen as the quantum leap in that respect. In the early 1980s, it did seem to be true that gaining this qualification brought about fairly instant financial and career rewards. But as MBAs have become less of a rarity, the attitude towards them is changing: for instance, the value of an MBA in the job market increasingly depends on where and when it was awarded. Furthermore, some kinds of employers attach more value than others to the intellectual qualities that an MBA course fosters.

It has also become clear that an MBA is of limited value in isolation. It has to be part of a wider career plan; otherwise it can easily lead those who possess it in the wrong direction. Equally, it is also only part of a wider view of training as such. Training is not a finite process, nor is it a question of boning up on 'flavour of the month' topics. It is the continuous process by which learning organizations renew themselves and the people who work in them.

Notes

1 C. Cox and C. Cooper, High flyers (Basil Blackwell, Oxford, 1988).
2 A. M. Souerwine, Career strategies (Amacom, New York, 1978).
3 The Times, 12 May 1988.
4 N. Nicholson and M. West, Managerial job change: men and women in transition (Cambridge University Press, 1988).
5 C. Handy, The age of unreason (Hutchinson, London, 1989).
6 Korn Ferry and Columbia School of Business, 21st century report: reinventing the CEO (New York and London).
7 P. Kakabadse and P. Dainty, Police chief officers, a management development survey (MCB University Press, Bradford, UK, 1988).
8 Personnel Today, 25 July 1989.

9 R. M. Kanter, *Men and women of the corporation* (Basic Books, New York, 1979).

10 J. J. Gabarro and J. P. Kotter, 'Managing your boss', *Harvard Business Review*, January–February 1980.

11 K. de Vries (Economist Intelligence Unit), 'Managers who drive their companies mad', *Multinational Business*, Spring 1987.

12 Kanter, *Men and women of the corporation*.

13 A bad way to be visible was described by another manager who told of an obnoxious younger eager beaver who used to leave messages on his superiors' desks which read 'Called by at 7.30 – sorry to have missed you'. He did not last long.

14 Kanter, *Men and women of the corporation*.

15 A. Jay, *Management and Machiavelli* (Hodder & Stoughton, London, 1967/ Penguin, London, 1970).

16 M. Korda, *Power! How to get it, how to use it* (Random House, New York/ Weidenfeld & Nicolson, London, 1975).

17 'Britain's most admired companies', *The Economist*, 9 September 1989.

18 *The Sunday Times*, 24 July 1988.

19 M. Korda, *Male chauvinism: how it works at home and in the office* (Simon & Schuster, New York/Coronet, London, 1972).

20 *Stuttgarter Zeitung*, 12 November 1988.

21 'Going to work on a weekend marriage', *The Times*, 2 August 1989.

22 R. M. Kanter, *When giants learn to dance* (Simon & Schuster, New York and London, 1989).

23 R. W. Baston, *The company-based MBA* (Harbridge House, London, 1989).

24 *The Sunday Times*, 11 June 1989.

25 K. Barham, J. Fraser and L. Heath, *Management for the future* (Ashridge Management College, Berkhamsted, Herts, UK, 1988).

11

Peaks, Plateaux and Slippery Slopes

The skill which mainly distinguishes knowledgeable investors from amateur punters on the stock market is knowing when to sell. The point was dramatically illustrated by Sir James Goldsmith when he liquidated his entire portfolio a few days before the great crash in October 1987. The successful managers we talked to seemed to have a similar instinct when it came to making career decisions. A typical example was the director of one of Britain's leading leisure conglomerates, whose career moves – quite unplanned, he said – had, by his mid-thirties, successively taken him into three major growth fields of business activity in the 1980s. For many people, though, it can be very difficult to move when there is no pressing need to do so. The attractions of familiarity with what it takes to do one's job well, the desire to see through current projects, the existence of supportive networks of friends and colleagues – all these are factors that make it hard to move, even when you feel you should. That is all the more true when the job carries with it considerations of money, status or power. Lee Iacocca, as President of the Ford Motor Company, was a prime example of someone who held on too long because of that. By the time he was sacked in 1978 there were plenty of signs that relations between himself and his chairman, Henry Ford, were cool, to say the least. But Iacocca was emotionally locked in to the excitement of launching new Ford products, while materially he had become accustomed to the lavish lifestyle which went with being the head of one of the world's biggest companies. Significantly, though, the biggest tie of all was financial. He was earning just under a million dollars a year and wanted to break the six-figure boundary. 'I wanted that $1 million a year, so much I couldn't face reality', he admits in his memoirs.

The money junkies

Money is a motivating factor in making career decisions, but excessive dependency upon it can be dangerous. Psychologist Tony Lake, some of whose ideas we described in chapter 4, says that power depends on how much choice is available to those over whom it is exercised: the more options that are open to them, the more difficult it becomes to force them to do things against their will or judgement. 'We've got them by the collaterals', a notoriously unlovable tycoon is reported to have said when someone asked him how he could get managers to stay with his company. He had made them dependent, and therefore put them at his mercy, by paying them large salaries and locking them into soft loans. The more lightly one travels, in terms of financial dependency, the easier it is to preserve one's freedom to make smart career moves.

Headhunters have pointed out that this is a particularly important principle for young MBAs to bear in mind at the start of their careers. It is also one that may affect other graduates when student loans come into operation in the UK. The natural temptation will be to head for jobs which pay high initial salaries to recover the costs of the course, but these may not constitute the best move in the long term. For instance, the highest starting salaries for bright graduates are in consultancy or financial services. But, as we remarked in the previous chapter, it is hard to make a switch from those sectors into line management once you reach thirtysomething. The obvious answer might be said to be to 'make your pile' in a high-reward job and then to move out into the more financially prosaic fields which lead to big-company line management. In practice, though, once one has got the money habit, it is extremely difficult to kick it. Often there are just too many hostages to fortune in the shape of large mortgages and a lifestyle to which one has become accustomed. The answer to the money junkie trap, headhunters say, is to keep an eye on long-term objectives. If your ultimate aim is to become chief executive of a major company, earning £250 000 or so a year, why spoil your chances for the sake of an extra few thousand in your twenties?

Equally, people making mid-career moves should look at more than the rewards attached to the job. In the USA, in fact, money is almost never mentioned in appointments advertisements at management level. It is the job specification that is paramount, and the assumption is that if the candidate's performance measures up, the rewards will follow. It is an example that could be followed advantageously in other countries, but in its absence our advice is that candidates should consider the long-term career implications of a job as well as the remuneration element. Cases in point, headhunters say, were the promising executives who went off in search of big rewards in the Middle East in the 1970s. When the boom petered out in the 1980s, they found their experience very hard to market back home. Today the problem is that of those who have been tempted by large financial inducements to move to a small-firm environment in mid-career. In most cases, they will very probably find it difficult to move back later into general management in a large company. If that is your ambition, the moves you make will have to be consistent with it.

The best way to ensure that job moves make sense is to have a career strategy which sets objectives in terms of industry or occupation, position, salary and career development over a certain timespan, but in real life most people are largely reactive, often in an almost subconscious way. There merely comes a point when they start reading the job advertisements and letting it be known, discreetly or otherwise, that they are available. What triggers such thoughts? If they are not under external pressure, it is one of those things that they are rather unsystematic about. It is rather like the 'vibes' you have about the look of an organization – a feeling you get that you cannot actually put into words. Nevertheless, there are classifiable slippery slopes on the career map and they have their own identifiable signposts by which they can be recognized. These fall into two groups – alarm bells and warning voices.

Alarm bells

Takeovers and mergers

Takeovers and mergers are top of the list, and the more senior you are, the greater the risk, especially in a hostile takeover. Warning that '"acquisitions fever" may well be the flavour of the next mid-decade', the London Business School conducted a survey of 100 predominantly uncontested takeovers in 1987.[1] The survey found that within a month, sellers' boards lost 16 per cent of their members, while over a quarter left within the first year. Newspaper reports and a great deal of anecdotal evidence also suggest that there is a considerable fall-out amongst managers below top level, as rationalization of functions and locations takes effect. However, the employee group that is most vulnerable is the one whose activities are closest to the interests of the company that has made the acquisition. For example, when a family-owned magazine publishing firm was taken over after an uncontested bid from a company with a very strong advertising bias, the advertising manager was asked to leave almost immediately. The editorial team were urged to stay on, because in that area the bidders felt much less sure of themselves.

The London Business School survey also showed that quite a number of employees at all levels eventually left, even though the bidder would have liked them to stay on. The reason for that is that a merger or takeover almost inevitably produces a culture clash between the two parties involved. There was much evidence of that in the City after Big Bang. Reporting one of the many mergers that took place at that time between clearing banks and merchant banks, *The Economist* described how some of the mainly public-school-educated managers of the latter sneered at the 'nylon suit and nine to five brigade' of the clearing banks.[2] At more senior levels, the complaint of the merchant bankers was that they were not sufficiently consulted on major decisions, which tended to be determined by clearing rather than merchant bank criteria. Many of them soon 'voted with their feet'. The point is that after a takeover, contested or otherwise, it is the culture of the company that made the bid that becomes dominant. The way we do things around here becomes the way they do things around there. The change can be very marked, especially when corporate cultures are reinforced by national cultural differences.

The arrival of a new boss

The arrival of a new boss, either from within the company or as an appointment from the outside, can threaten the position of those who are currently in place. Often the person appointed will want to bring at least some members of his or her team with them, either as a support system or because it is difficult to make changes when the existing management group has become used to doing things their way.

One of the dangers of having a sponsor or mentor is that it leaves the person being sponsored vulnerable to changes of this kind. The Ashridge College report on *Women in management*, to which we have previously referred, makes the point that this is a particular problem for women. They found that 'Without exception, the women we spoke to stressed the importance of having a mentor – generally a male colleague at a higher level'. But one consequence of that was that their situation could deteriorate very rapidly if the mentor left. The high-flyers interviewed by Cooper and Cox said they owed a lot to intervention by mentors and sponsors at important points in their careers, but they stressed that they were careful not to tie themselves to any one individual. It was not a planned strategy – just one of the ways in which that group instinctively get it right. But we can all learn from the successful instincts of others – corporate Darwinism.

A more straightforward threat comes about when the new boss is a former colleague with whom previous relationships had been adversarial. Two managers with whom we spoke had been forced into an untenable position within weeks of being passed over by a former rival.

Trouble at t'mill

The *Titanic* is said to have sunk with lights blazing and the band playing to first-class passengers in evening dress. No one knows whether this was a supreme example of *sang froid* or whether they simply did not know what was happening. The fact is that when you are in the middle of a developing disaster, it is often quite difficult to find out what is going on. That is true of sinking companies as well as sinking ships.

However, a large firm, especially one with strong asset backing and well diversified activities, can take a long time to go under and is most likely to become the subject of a bid well before then. For an older manager, the best course of action may well be to hang on until retirement or to hope for an eventual golden handshake from a successful bidder. But for those in early or mid-career, the risk of waiting in the doldrums for a pay-off from a rich white knight is probably not worth taking. There is also the further danger that an individual activity may simply be shut down or sold off.

The trouble is that managers are often too busy, too loyal, or, it must be said, too frightened of moving to take action. A leading career consultant urges, however, that they should make a practice of 'walking the deck' every now and then, especially if they have a gut feeling that everything is not as it should be. The most common indicators of trouble include:

- A continuing decline in profits or adverse factors in key ratios
- Creative accounting: an early sign of trouble in one firm, for instance, was when overheads were piled on to one of its subsidiaries in order to make its core activity look healthier than it was in reality
- Slow payment of suppliers
- Lack of investment in new plant or the maintenance of buildings and facilities: this is a warning sign for the organization as a whole or for a particular activity – in the latter case it is usually a preliminary to a close-down
- Unrealistic financial projections
- High staff turnover, particularly the departure of key people
- Adverse press comment

Money

The majority of private-sector companies have abandoned incremental pay (more or less automatic rises, based on grades) in favour of performance-related schemes. These are designed to send executives 'messages' about what the organization's management feels about their performance. Ideally, they should be accompanied by personally conducted appraisals, but the extent to which superiors are prepared to be frank in such encounters, or to give totally honest reports in writing, varies. However, the message in the annual salary review is usually unambiguous. If you are falling behind your peer group, or the income targets you have set yourself, it is time to think about moving on.

Warning voices

Corporate sclerosis

This is a common disease of entrepreneurially owned companies when the founder runs out of steam. The symptoms have been well described by Paul Thorne in one of his *International Management* articles:[3]

> As the entrepreneur's company grows, so the seeds of its eventual failure begin to find fertile ground. The more successful the entrepreneur, the more convinced he becomes of his own infallibility, the more unwilling he is to listen to criticism, and the less he understands the conditions necessary for his company's continuing survival. . . . To work with the successful entrepreneur you need to be acutely aware of when it is time to cut and run.

In that same article, Thorne also warns against another symptom of impending sclerosis which particularly affects family businesses – nepotism. There have been cases in which businesses have been successfully passed on within a family, but they are outnumbered by those that merely reinforce the saying that blood is thicker than water. The crucial question is whether the family succession would have taken place on merit. If not, the longer-term future of the organization is problematical.

Boredom with the job

Talking to managers whose careers have come adrift, one of the consistent themes that emerges is that they knew in their heart of hearts that they were no longer performing at the standards of which they knew they were capable. They had ceased to enjoy what they were doing and were no longer devoting the same care and attention to it as they once did. Instead, some were taking too long over lunch, while others were more involved in fringe activities than in the job itself. At the same time, they had settled at a comfort level at which they rejected the thought of change. The crucial question to ask yourself in these circumstances is this: Would you hire yourself for the job you are now doing, if you were a third party? Unless the answer is a clear affirmative, it is time to consider your position.

Lack of opportunity for training and self-development

As we have said in earlier chapters, it is an absolutely vital aspect of career management to keep your skills up to date and to widen their range as much as possible. If the organization fails to provide the right opportunities for this, it either does not regard you as a good long-term investment, or it is the wrong place to be, certainly for someone under 45.

The need to update skills never ceases, even for senior managers, because there is a de-skilling aspect to management itself. In focusing heavily on the *being* aspect of a function, you lose sight of the other constituent, the *doing* one. It begins to vanish over the horizon as you get further away from the requirement to exercise it on a daily basis. That was the hard lesson learned by a 46-year-old main board member of a major company, for whom he had worked for some 20 years. He resigned after a clash with its new managing director, and thought there would be little difficulty in getting another job. But events turned out otherwise:

> At first I thought my age was the reason I was being rejected by various companies who I had been confident would offer me something. I had a pretty good track record, was fairly well

known by a number of key players in my industry and had been actively involved in getting some extremely successful ventures off the ground. But then I realised, and I must say it was with a sinking heart, that my knowledge was very company-specific and that there were huge gaps in it. When I was in my thirties managers didn't go on training courses much. Later on I always had too much to do for the company to send me off to learn some of the things I should have known more about. For instance, I hadn't ever got to grips with information technology – the people working for me handled all that. I didn't have any really up to date technical knowledge and I hadn't actually *done* anything of a hands-on nature for years. I'd been a manager, primarily in a strategy role and when I was pressed in interviews on the extent of my line experience, I didn't come out too well.

This extremely intelligent man, fluent in several languages, did eventually get another job, in which he has been outstandingly successful, but he first had to endure many anxious months of unemployment.

Typecasting

Being typecast as 'the expert in . . .' can be a deadly career trap for those who have broader career ambitions. It is, of course, very beguiling, because 'experts in . . .' are doing what they like best and are best at. That may be the perfectly legitimate limit to your aims but it makes you vulnerable when the time comes at which your expertise is no longer quite so necessary or when it is overtaken by technology. That is what happened to some highly paid EDP managers in the 1980s, when the demand for programming was lessened by the advent of a huge variety of ready-made software packages.

To some extent, the answer is to keep renewing skills through training, but if the 'expert in . . .' wants to move on to other roles in the organization, he or she may either find that they are considered to be too valuable in their present function or that they strike the over-specialization syndrome, described by two American organization watchers, Ritti and Funkhouse:[4]

> Look at John Wayne. What if he had been cast as a thug or as a werewolf. Who would believe it? Who would watch the movie without saying 'What's that cowboy doing, sprouting hair and claws when the moon is high?'

Siberias and sidetracks

In every organization, there are functions and activities which have the reputation of being dead ends. They are the ones from which people rarely get promoted because they do not provide visibility or because the guardians of the dominant culture regard them as unimportant, or which actually are unimportant from an objective point of view; for example, in a company whose market was primarily a domestic one the job of export manager, however styled, would not be of much consequence. But dead ends can also be found in areas that are or ought to be functionally important. In the later 1970s or early 1980s, personnel management fell out of favour and became associated with a 'welfare-state' mentality that was by then very unpopular with senior management.

That, however, illustrates a curious point about 'Siberias': they can also be lands of opportunity. In its new guise of 'human resource management', personnel has become a key role as people, rather than plant, are becoming the crucial assets of many organizations. Customer service is another classic example. The emphasis on 'closeness to the customer' as a source of competitive edge has made this once-lowly area a stopover for fast-trackers. The same is true of export sales, until recently the Cinderella of the marketing department of many British and US companies.

Plateauing

As we said in the first chapter, plateauing has had a bad press, but it is a career phenomenon of which we will be seeing much more as organizations change their shape from ladders to flat pyramids. A report on the subject produced by the Industrial Training Research Unit of Sundridge Park Management Centre, based on a sample of 20 large companies in a variety of fields, showed that as many as 50 per cent of their managers were regarded as plateaued.

Some of these were young former high-flyers who, for one reason or another, had made wrong career moves. Others were specialists who had fallen into the 'expert in . . .' trap. For these two groups the best move would appear to be a job change, although that suggestion takes us back to the question of evaluating what one's own real aims and objectives are and whether these are realistic. It is perfectly possible to have a satisfying career and personal development experience on the plateaux of flat-pyramid organizations. Some younger managers recognize this by looking, quite rightly, at whether the content and scope of the job provides that, rather than where it is in the hierarchy. For instance, in the career development seminars that are given to ICI executives at the company's Billingham plant, it has turned out that many highly qualified young managers are more interested in ways of enhancing job satisfaction than in getting on the board.

It is an example that those past the thirtysomething barrier, who constitute the majority of plateaued managers, might well consider. Plateauing is merely a sign that they have exhausted the possibilities of a particular table of job contents. The crucial question, from a career point of view, is whether they are interested in broadening its scope and whether the organization will allow them to do that.

There are, quite frankly, cultures who operate an 'up or out' rule: these are usually small-firm person or power cultures such as professional practices. At the other end of the scale are organizations who pretend that the problem of plateauing does not exist, and who allow plateaued executives to go into a kind of psychological retirement. That is a luxury which firms are increasingly unable to afford and is therefore a dangerous position to get into. It is there that the axe falls when the time comes to make cutbacks, and it is also the most difficult career course to explain when looking for a job later.

The healthy organizational attitude to the plateauing problem is that which an article in *Management Today* has termed 'integrative'.[5] Integrative organizations consider how individual objectives can be fitted into the future of the organization, have a view of what skills are needed over the longer period, have training for everybody, not just the stars and high-flyers, and review and monitor individual progress against agreed goals.

Intrapreneuring

A plateau can become a highly visible jumping-off place for a subsequent career move if it becomes a base for intrapreneurship. Intrapreneuring – the development of entrepreneurial activities within, rather than outside, the organization – has become a fashionable concept in recent years. It is seen as a highly effective agent of change and product innovation. Some companies with a strong task culture – 3M is the example most often quoted – actively encourage it by allowing their managers a time and money budget for their own pet projects, for which they are also allowed to use corporate facilities. For example, 3M's Post-it notes, the little yellow pads with a peel-off adhesive top found in almost every stationery shop in the world, are the fruits of an intrapreneurial venture by a 3M employee who, at the time, was a relatively junior research technician. However, intrapreneuring is not age-related. 'While intrapreneurs tend to be young, many are also in midlife career crisis or are nearing retirement', writes Gifford Pinchot, the author of the standard work on the subject.[6]

Intrapreneurs have many career anchors in common with entrepreneurs, though they are less concerned with ownership of the outcome of what they do. In using the financial and technical resources of the organization that employs them, they sacrifice many of the direct rewards of entrepreneurship in exchange for a greater degree of security. That can create problems later on if they start to look for a direct pay-off on a venture that has made a lot of money for their company – which is one of the factors that budding intrapreneurs ought to take into account. The post-feudal organization is not noted for acts of generosity unless it is contractually bound to them.

Very few organizations have a formal programme for sponsoring intrapreneurship. Mostly it just happens as a result of an initiative by an individual manager, and often one who has been plateaued. A good example was observed by one of us back in the 1960s, long before intrapreneuring entered the language of management literature.

As manager of the London office of a leading American publishing company, he was reporting to Theo, the head of its international division in New York. Theo was an extremely bright but somewhat idiosyncratic man who, in his early forties, was clearly not going to get further in the company. The international division, which accounted for only 2 per cent of the company's turnover, was something of a dumping ground for people the company didn't want to fire, but also didn't quite know how to use.

One of the problems faced by the international division at the time was that American textbooks were considerably more expensive than British ones and here Theo hit on a good idea. By reprinting some of the company's standard texts in the Far East – at that time Japan was a low-cost economy – they could be brought out at a much lower price, and still show a large profit margin. There were a few technical and legal problems to be overcome, but after solving those Theo got the go-ahead for a venture that soon proved to be hugely successful and which came to be widely imitated by his competitors. He left the company when it was taken over some time later and became a partner in a venture that was an indirect product of his original idea.

Theo was not a business school product; quite the reverse. He was a shrewd, old-style, seat-of-the-pants manager who instinctively grasped the principles of what it takes to initiate an intrapreneurial venture in a somewhat bureaucratic (role culture) organization with a heavy complement of 'no'-saying middle management:

- He happened to be in what has been termed 'a corridor of indifference'. No one much cared about the international

division and he had designed his venture in such a way that it
was not going to involve hiring extra people or making extra
work for anybody who was not directly involved in it.

- He had anticipated possible technical and legal objections and
worked out the answers to them.
- With the help of a powerful ally, an extremely able young
executive in the company treasurer's office, he had costed the
venture and put forward profit projections. Nobody quite
believed them, but the downside risk was modest in relation to
the volume of business his division was doing. He also established a set of cashflow projections which ensured that the
venture could not become a bottomless investment sink.
- He had worked out the marketing and distribution logistics of
the operation.

In other words, intrapreneurs are not just individuals with a bright
idea. They work that idea up to full business plan presentation
standards and have the experience and the will to implement it.
They are 'dreamers who do', a rare breed which all organizations
look for, no matter where their previous career has taken them.

Going out on a limb – the second career

True entrepreneurs move to a different rhythm from those whose
careers are bound to organizations. They mostly start young, early
in their twenties, although there is a school of thought which
advocates working in an organization first – in order to make your
early mistakes at someone else's expense. A further window of
opportunity for entrepreneurship has opened up in recent years
for the thirtysomethings, through the vogue for management buy-
outs, which has made it relatively easy for young managers to raise
money to buy divested parts of the companies for whom they
have been working. But in general you are unlikely to be supple
enough to catch the beat of the entrepreneurial drum past your
mid-forties. So does that mean that if, by then, it has become clear
that you are not going to reach your career objectives, there is
nothing left to do but to play out time?

Certainly this used often to be the case in the days when careers were long-term commitments to perhaps only two or three organizations in the course of a working lifetime. The post-feudal relationship between masters and men or women has changed all that. To continue the games metaphor, the danger now is that you may be substituted before the end to make room for those who can run on to the field fresh, so it is important to prepare, well ahead of the event, for possible courses of action for the last 20 years or so of working life. Indeed, it is quite possible that a very large section of the management population, irrespective of their roles and of the kind of cultures in which these are enacted, will have to think about their careers in those terms. So will their employers. This is because an increasing number of commentators agree with Professor Charles Handy's view that the speed and high pressures of social and techno-logical change may mean that careers at what he calls the 'organ-izational core' will only last for 20 or 25 years. In his book, *The age of unreason*, he writes:[7]

The core workers will have a harder but shorter job, with more people leaving full time employment in their late forties or early fifties, partly because they no longer want the pressures that such jobs will increasingly entail, but mainly because there will be younger, more qualified and more energetic people available for those core jobs.

But where will the opportunities for second careers be? One point that Handy has not made is that a lot of people who have been reasonably successful in their core roles will have accumu-lated quite substantial capital sums in the form of share options. They will also be at a stage in their lives when direct financial com-mitments to children's education, mortgages and so forth will have diminished. Those two factors combine to open up a second set of career options in two ways. Firstly, having a solid capital base removes or diminishes the search to fulfil basic needs in favour of higher ones for self-actualization. Secondly, it increases freedom of action by making you less vulnerable to those who can 'get you by the collaterals'.

The outcome takes people in different directions. One interesting piece of evidence comes from those who recruit managers for charities. They report a very significant amount of interest from executives who have reached a stage at which they are contemplating second careers in which they want, in a current phrase, 'to put something back into the community'. Charity salaries, although higher than they once were, are lower than in the commercial world, but former core managers are in the position of being able to afford to take jobs that augment a pension rather than being a key source of income.

Another area of opportunity is highlighted in Handy's book. 'If the core is smaller', he asks, 'who then does the work? Increasingly it is contracted out'. There is already a huge growth in various forms of freelance consultancy, which enables organizations flexibly to link the know-how of older managers with the energy and enthusiasm of the younger members of their core workforce. It is a method of working which organizations have yet to learn to manage systematically, just as the providers of these services have to learn to define and market their expertise. But with the emerging skills shortage, there is no doubt that the potential demand exists. Already some 'retired' executives are reporting that they are busier, and in some cases earning more, as consultants than they were as employees. For second careers which begin in the third age we suspect that this may be a smarter move into the enterprise culture than the stress and financial commitment of a full-scale entrepreneurial involvement.[8]

Executive summary

One of the key skills of career self-management is knowing when to move on. High-flyers have an instinct for it, although their status can also make them vulnerable to getting caught in the money trap. The highest offer in money terms only makes sense in the context of an overall career plan. This is as true in making a mid-career move as it is for newly minted MBAs. The content of the job, what it is likely to lead to and what it provides in the way of management development is at least as important as the financial rewards that go with it. The idea that short-term, income-maximizing moves can be made with the intention of a sub-sequent switch into mainstream line management is apt to be delusion, because a high income is habit forming. Dependence upon money will seriously limit your freedom to make voluntary career moves.

But what does prompt people to make such moves? High-flyers make them because they see windows of opportunity. Others react to a variety of what are mostly gut feelings. However, it is possible to classify a variety of situations which should cause one to evaluate the possibilities of making a move. Some are direct threats such as the consequences of a takeover or indications that an organization is on the decline. Others, equally dangerous, take the form of warning signs to which people are often tempted to turn a blind eye, such as boredom with a job which one is conscious of not doing as well as one once did, lack of opportunity for training and development, or a feeling of having reached a point in the organizational hierarchy from which one is not likely to progress further.

The last aspect is known as plateauing, and it is becoming increasingly common as the shape of organizations changes from multi-runged ladders into flat pyramids. For ambitious young high-flyers the crucial question is whether, when that point has been reached, their view of themselves is still realistic in their own eyes. If it is, a career plateau is a sign that there is a discrepancy between their estimation of themselves and that which the organization has of them. In that case they should try their luck elsewhere. For others, the crucial question about a plateau is how wide it is or can be made to become. There are many ways in which the content of a job can be expanded to become the basis of a satisfying and stable career. Whether that is possible in practice depends on the organization as well as the individual. Organizations that recognize the reality of plateauing, and plan appropriate career paths for people who have reached a structural limit, are better – and more secure – places to work in than those who ignore the phenomenon or allow it to turn into a form of psychological retirement.

One of the ways of broadening a mid-career plateau is intra-preneuring; developing the job along entrepreneurial lines but using the organization's resources. Carried out successfully, it can turn a plateau into a springboard.

One of the features that distinguishes intrapreneuring from entrepreneuring is that it is not age-related. True entrepreneurs, those who start and build up their own businesses, begin young. Most people, as they grow older, simply lack the time, energy, will and motivation for this. For older managers who break away, the best course is to find ways of linking their wisdom to the energy of organizational cores, or to find areas where their expertise can serve the needs of the community as a whole. The skills shortage of the 1990s is already opening up a variety of opportunities of this nature.

Notes

1 J. W. Hunt, S. Lees, J. J. Grumbar and P. D. Vivian, *Acquisitions, the human factor* (London Business School and Egon Zehnder International, London, 1987).

2 *The Economist*, 22 October 1988.

3 P. Thorne, *International Management*, December 1988.

4 R. Ritti and G. Funkhouse, *The ropes to skip and the ropes to pull* (John Wiley, New York and Chichester, 1987).

5 B. Bartlett, 'The bypassed manager', *Management Today*, June 1987.

6 G. Pinchot, *Intrapreneuring* (Harper & Row, New York and London, 1985).

7 C. Handy, *The age of unreason* (Hutchinson, London, 1989).

8 G. Golzen, *Going Freelance* (Kogan Page, London, 1989).

12

Smart Moves for the Twenty-first Century

A survey of young high-flyers in their twenties and thirties on how they envisaged the business environment in the year 2000 warned that 'the only accurate prediction about the future is that most of the predictions are likely to be wrong'.[1] At the beginning of the 1980s, for instance, who would have predicted the course of events in Russia and Eastern Europe towards the end of that decade? Nevertheless, it is possible to look at present trends and say that, if things go on in the same way, they are likely to have a certain, roughly predictable set of outcomes. The objective of this chapter is to discuss these, to show what impact they might have on careers in the twenty-first century and how that might also affect career decisions in the short term.

The demographic effect

We now know that every European Community country, except Ireland, will show a sharp drop in the numbers of school leavers entering the job market in the 1990s, and that there is a similar, if smaller, trend in Japan and the USA. We also know that this will inevitably produce a shortage of graduates and, ultimately, of managers. It is greater in some countries than others, but the demand for people with degrees or equivalent qualifications will continue to grow everywhere throughout the 1990s.[2] This is particularly true in science, technology and the professions, but even those with apparently 'useless' qualifications, such as degrees in history or English literature, will be pulled in to fill the gaps. For example, accountancy firms, who recruit around 11 per cent of all graduates entering first employment for their training programmes, do not require them to have a relevant degree (e.g. in business, economics or a numerical discipline) or even to be particularly numerate. Similarly, some far-seeing employers in the technology field, such as Hewlett-Packard, are taking on arts graduates and training them to become computer-literate.

At the other end of the age scale, there are widespread predictions that older managers and professionals will be brought back into the workforce and that the days of early retirement may be coming to end, at least in the sense of dropping out into inactivity at 55 or so. Apart from the skills shortage, another powerful reason that is being advanced is that those in work will simply not be able to finance the retirement pensions of the growing army of not-so-senior citizens.[3]

What we are already seeing, as a result of demographics, is the leading edge of a very strong sellers' market for those who can make a contribution to the economy. It is one that employers will increasingly try to buy into early by offering sponsorship to students. In fact, in the UK this is already happening on a larger scale than is often realized. In 1989–90, for instance, GEC–Marconi alone offered over 600 sponsorships to engineering and computer studies students, and there are many similar schemes in operation, particularly in engineering.

Inducements to finance studies with money from a future employer are bound to increase and spread to other desirable disciplines with the switch from higher education grants to student loans, but they may include a career catch. At present the majority of sponsorships do not carry with them any contractual obligation to join the company that has provided the money, but that situation may change if their financial involvement becomes larger and the skill shortage becomes more pronounced. Shareholders, quite simply, may demand a human resource return on their investment in training. Even if there is no legal obligation tied into such an arrangement, the moral pressures to repay one's sponsor somehow can be made quite strong.

Sponsorship, and the need to repay student loans from other

sources, could – if they are not careful – push more graduates into the career trap that is at present faced by some MBAs: to make moves that are driven by external obligations, rather than by what they really want to do, who they really want to spend time with and what they feel they are best at. Some of the lessons in this book about investigating the culture of organizations at particular phases of their development and aligning that with one's own needs, values and career anchors may need to be applied early on – even at the stage of deciding whether or not to accept sponsorship from an organization that is offering it. A seller's market for talent and qualifications is a good one in which to be asking awkward questions from potential employers, particularly about the extent to which they offer continuing learning and career development opportunities.

An ascendancy of experts

We do not know if there is a collective noun for experts, but 'an ascendancy' could be an apt one for the twenty-first century, because the organizational trend that has been most widely singled out is that the accumulation of knowledge and expertise is becoming more important than movement up the hierarchy, except at the very top. The reasons are complex and are the result of a kind of loop that is produced by the revolutionary growth of information technology.

Information technology both speeds up the process of change and creates a demand for change. As only one of a myriad of examples, we mentioned in the first chapter how EPOS (electronic point of sale) technology enables retailers to record daily changes in patterns of demand on as many parameters as they care to build into the system. That in turn puts pressure on manufacturers to respond very quickly; which feeds back into carrying low inventories of materials and relying on 'just in time' methods. These again depend on information technology.

At the same time the availability of that technology throughout organizations eliminates the need for what Drucker calls 'boosters' – hierarchical levels whose job it is to filter, process and distribute information. Knowledge, or expertise, is the source of power, but the urgency of quick responses to information also means that it has to be orchestrated in different ways, by putting together teams of experts in various configurations to tackle constantly and rapidly changing sets of conditions. Single organizations, says Tom Peters, are giving way to co-operative networks.[4] The career lesson of that emerges from a comment by the perceptive futurologist Norman Macrae, in his farewell feature as deputy editor of *The Economist*:[5]

> The race to replace everything the EPOS shows to be fading will change the whole idea of career structures. No youngster entering a big corporation today should dream of being corporate Vice President by age 50. When he is 50, corporate bureaucracies should hardly exist.

The manager of the future, says Drucker, will be like the conductor of an orchestra of many talents. But he also draws another telling parallel to explain the relationship between managers and experts in the organization of the future. He takes the example of surgeons and specialists in a hospital. They also form teams to tackle specific operations. The specialist with the greatest area of expertise in a certain field will act as the leader, but at other times he or she will only be the adviser, and leadership will pass to the person whose expertise is most relevant to the task in hand. He writes: 'Much of the work is done in *ad hoc* teams, as required by an individual patient's diagnosis and condition'.[6]

Managers and administrators play a parallel role in all this which we shall come to shortly, but if we accept Drucker's model and see some truth in Norman Macrae's challenging generalization, the inference is that specialization is vital in career building for the future. The changing relationship of managers and specialists is reflected in an interesting discussion that we had with Caroline Paxton, a former Sandhurst instructor and now a management consultant. She made the point that the latest generation of helicopters are virtually flying computers, and the pilot, brave person though he or she needs to be over the target area, is utterly dependent upon specialists to get him or her there and to enable the mission to be fulfilled. One result of the new status of specialists is that pilots are expected to carry out some of the routine maintenance and cleaning tasks, which they used to regard as the more lowly province of technicians and mechanics.

The qualifications which create specialists and experts are not forever, which is why it is so important for organizations to create formal and informal[7] opportunities for learning; and for individuals to ensure that employment contracts are also development contracts with such opportunities built into them. But why should organizations invest time and money towards creating the circumstances that will enable people to make smart moves, possibly to a competitor organization who will cash in on their investment? One reason may be that market forces will not give them any option if they want to attract the people they most need. Another may be that they will find ways of recouping their investment. There may, for instance, be a clause in the employment contract which obliges employees to refund the costs of training, if they leave within a certain length of time. Another possibility that is being mooted is that employees will have a transfer value, rather like footballers. That value will include the cost of training, and when they move voluntarily most of it will accrue to the organization that provided it, as in football it goes mostly to the club that acquired, or discovered and nurtured, the talent in question. On the other hand, it is also possible that organizations will be providing training on such a wide scale in the twenty-first century that they will regard the loss of those who have been trained rather as accountancy practices now do. They look on the movement of accountants between practices as a question of swings and roundabouts, but regard the task of keeping their best people by providing an attractive career path for them as one of the essential tasks of management.

However, actually managing that path and making sure it really exists is an individual responsibility. Those who want to get out of the 'expert in . . .' trap that we referred to in the previous chapter will need to make sure that at least the range of their expertise is widened and that it does not become too organization-specific. They will also have to ensure that their contribution is made visible. Charles Handy has made the interesting suggestion that experts ought to be able to sign their work, as they sign their contribution in film credits, or as members of the building team are credited on building site placards. Making sure that credit is given where it is due may also be a feature of employment contracts in the twenty-first century.

What about the managers?

The people who run the organizations of the future will be experts whose career moves have taken them out of their speciality into general management and ultimately into chief executive roles. But instead of a steady progress up the corporate ladder, typically moving out of their speciality into managing units of increasing size, they will be making strategic additions to their expertise. These may involve sideways moves across the flat layers of the corporate pyramid along the lines we indicated in chapter 10: strategy, marketing, human resource management and corporate finance.

Some of the consultants whom we interviewed believed that, for future CEOs, marketing might be the most important of these experiences. That view is borne out by a *Sunday Times* report on the growing demand for marketers among big companies looking for potential high-flyers.[8] The reason, they explain, is that marketing, which is concerned with establishing goals and identifying opportunities, and then developing strategies, internally and externally, to reach them, is the practical core of the quality that leaders of organizations will increasingly need to have – vision.

It is a tough word to define, except by Drucker's analogy of the role of the conductor. He compares the various experts in the organization to musicians in an orchestra. They all have their instruments to play and are extremely good at playing them. But the quality of their total performance relies on the conductor's interpretation of the score. In corporate terms, that is the vision which has to be transmitted both to those at the core of the organization and those who, in increasing numbers, work at its periphery: contractors, part-timers, freelancers and consultants.

His analogy also suggests, incidentally, that the actual level of purely technical expertise in any one field may not be all that important for top management. Few conductors have been more than competent instrumentalists, and it is interesting to note that in Korn Ferry's survey of the ten qualities most required by CEOs in the twenty-first century, *doing* skills in technology, production and computer literacy ranked as the last three below others that called for *being* attributes. There is a connection between this finding and those of another survey, concerned with the qualities likely to be required of what it called 'Euro-executives'. Specific technical competencies, it says, are less important than the *being* attributes of flexibility, adaptability and a broad cultural empathy.[9]

But where does all this leave the functional or discipline specialists who are not bound for the top? Here Drucker's other analogy, that of the hospital, is illuminating, although one might easily take the example of a professional practice. Professionals do not like administration, in fact they do not like to do things which distract them from what they regard as their core tasks. Yet someone has to make sure that these tasks get done; for instance, that the right people arrive in the right place at the right time with the right equipment. Information technology can facilitate these processes, but ultimately they are a human responsibility. Organizations are increasingly recognizing that they discard 'faithful low-flyers', as an article in *The Times* has called them, at their peril.

The colour of money

Young managers in the 1960s and 1970s, when pay was tied to seniority of age and position – the two often coincided – used to argue, half-jokingly, that the pay pyramid was upside down. You ought to get paid more when you were young enough to enjoy it, when your immediate financial needs to pay mortgages and childrens' education were greater and when your input of energy was very high, and less later on. Something like this could well happen, at least in the relative reward positions of specialists and general managers. Traditionally, the big rewards have gone to the generalists; for instance, engineers in the UK have always been badly paid in comparison to their colleagues on what used to be called 'the management side'.

The sellers' market in talent, plus the new perceptions about the importance of specialists, which we referred to in the section about their ascendancy, are changing all this. Indeed, the reward systems of organizations may become more like those in a football club, where stars are paid at least as much as the manager and much more than those who provide support functions, such as coaching or physiotherapy.

However, at the moment, all sectors of organizations are paid much better in real terms than a decade or two ago, and (allowing for inflation) many thirtysomethings are earning sums that their counterparts of that time would have looked on with envy and even incredulity. But there is a price to pay for this, and it is one that we see in the post-feudal relationship between masters and men or women to which we referred in the first chapter. Organizations will pay a great deal of money to get and keep the talents they want. But they will work them extremely hard, and they will not feel any obligation to pay for them once they no longer want them. Even though the best and most caring of employers will try to find other outlets for those for whom time has run out in various ways, Charles Handy warns that future full-time careers at the cores of organizations may only last for 20 or 25 years, except for those who get to the top. Since that already happens in the armed forces, where even people who get almost to the top as two-star generals (or as their naval and air force equivalents) have to retire in their early fifties, his forecast seems a likely one, especially given the pace and scale of change in the organizational world as a whole.

Careers in the third age

The positive side of the shortening of full-time careers is that, while they are going on, they are increasingly very well paid. They also offer the opportunity to build up large capital sums through share option schemes. For example, a 1989 survey of directors' shareholdings in The Sunday Times[10] showed that 200 directors had shareholdings in their companies worth £10 m or more – the bulk were worth between £15 m and £30 m. Admittedly, some of these were owner–entrepreneurs, but it seems likely that corresponding benefits extended quite widely down the organization.

In the course of this book, we have talked more about the self-development aspect of moves than about reward, but reward is also important as a long-term objective because it determines the power one has to choose among a number of third-age career options in which rewards will be less, but the chance to realize personal needs will be greater. For some, these will occur within the organizations themselves, in areas such as training, coaching and mentoring. These will appeal to those who continue to have strong career anchors in security and affiliation. For those who are attracted to causes, there are growing opportunities for work in charities; some of which are already big businesses in their own right and pay salaries which, although lower than in the business world, are much above the honorarium levels of a few years ago. Teaching and various forms of work in the community are also likely to open up as avenues of third-age employment, as it becomes harder to find enough young people to fill vacancies in these sectors.

For those who have reached a point at which, after years in an organizational setting, autonomy has become their aim, the growth of subcontracting and freelance work opens up areas of scope for self-employment that hardly existed in the early 1980s. But here, as elsewhere in this book, the starting point is self-recognition. Knowing where you start is always the essential preliminary to smart moves.

Notes

1 The Cookham Group, *Headlines 2000: the world as we see it* (Hay Management Consultants, London, 1988).
2 R. Pearson and G. Pike, *The graduate labour market in the 1990s* (Institute of Manpower Studies, Brighton, UK, 1989).
3 'They've got to eat, so let them work', *The Economist*, 16 September 1989.
4 Tom Peters, 'Tomorrow's companies', *The Economist*, 4 March 1989.
5 Norman Macrae, 'The next ages of man', *The Economist*, 24 December 1988.

6 Peter Drucker, 'The coming of the new organisation', *Harvard Business Review*, January–February 1988.

7 In an article in *International Management* entitled 'Do it yourself career development is the order of the 90s', Paul Thorne suggests what these might be: 'training course, home-working provisions, sabbaticals, buy-ins and buy-outs, departmental, corporate and international transfers, part-time MBAs, personal counselling, parallel career planning for dual career families, job sampling, job sharing, flexible compensation packages ...'.

8 'Marketers head for the boardroom', *The Sunday Times*, 24 September 1989.

9 *The search for the Euro-executive* (Saxton Bampfylde International, London, 1989).

10 *The Sunday Times*, 17 September 1989.

Index

Index compiled by Meg Davies (Society of Indexers)